Athletic Throwing

Athletic Throwing

by PETER TANCRED
and CYRIL A. CARTER

FABER AND FABER
London   Boston

First published in 1980
by Faber and Faber Limited
3 Queen Square London WC1N 3AU
Set, printed and bound in Great Britain by
Fakenham Press Limited, Fakenham, Norfolk
All rights reserved

British Library Cataloguing in Publication Data

Tancred, Peter
  Athletic Throwing.
  1. Weight throwing.
  I. Title II. Carter, Cyril A
  796.4′35   GV1091

  ISBN 0–571–11479–2

Contents

ACKNOWLEDGEMENTS   6

FOREWORD by MAC WILKINS   7

INTRODUCTION   9

I. PREPARATION TRAINING   11

II. DISCUS   31

III. SHOT   57

IV. HAMMER   81

V. JAVELIN   105

Peter Tancred's Competitive Career   126

Acknowledgements
and Dedication

To: David Finch for his excellent photography; Ron Wyld for the splendid graphic illustrations; John Davies, Director of the Crystal Palace National Sports Centre, for the use of the facilities; Adidas (UK) Ltd for their sponsorship; Tony Bulfield (Dunlop Ltd); Bob Roberts, Wolverhampton and Bilston Athletic Club; Mac Wilkins, friend, and author of the foreword to this book.

Our thanks also to: John le Mesurier (BAAB Principal National Coach), Wilf Paish (BAAB National Coach), Howard Payne (Hammer), and Mike Winch (Shot) for their advice and technical assistance in the compilation of this book.

We further wish to thank the Sports Aid Foundation (S.A.F.).

We should like to dedicate this book to the following:

To my wife, Rita, for her appreciation and understanding, and the typing of the manuscript; (Cyril)

To my father for providing the initial technical advice and assistance, and to my mother for endowing me with good health;

To Liz for her patience, understanding and support;

To Mr C. K. Lipton for his advice and friendship. (Peter)

Foreword

by Mac Wilkins (USA), World Discus Record Holder and greatest all-round thrower.

It is with great pleasure that I write the foreword to this book on Athletic Throwing. Good books on the 'Cinderella' events of athletics are very rare indeed and this book will undoubtedly go a long way to ensure a better understanding and appreciation of these events.

Peter Tancred, British Champion and Olympic Discus Thrower, and one of Britain's best all-round throwers, has combined with his Coach Cyril Carter, former Olympic Gymnast and lecturer in Human Movement Studies, to write this valuable contribution to material on athletics. Although, by necessity, this book provides information on techniques specifically suited to Peter Tancred, it is invaluable in that it provides information, not only about basic fundamentals, but on how such fundamentals are adapted to suit the individual in order to produce optimum performance. The parts of this book that are devoted to preparation training are unique in that they provide equal emphasis on considerations other than merely strength and size, which have in the past been regarded as the only prerequisites for athletes engaged in throwing events.

Pete's technical excellence at the sport, plus his knowledge and ability to communicate his expertise, means that this book will promote success for all athletes who practise throwing. Cyril, despite not having been a thrower himself, undoubtedly brings a valuable critical perspective to this work with his ability, resulting from his athletics coaching and gymnastics training, to recognize body movement.

Athletic Throwing is one of the oldest Olympic activities that is practised by men, women and children world-wide. I believe that this book will encourage further participation and achievement in this deeply rewarding sport.

MAC WILKINS

Introduction

Because of the assortment of contrasting styles currently employed by the world's leading throwers, it should be stressed that it is not our intention to suggest that the techniques described in this book are the only ones which will bring success. Athletic throwing events, although seemingly static in form, are by no means stagnant in the progress of techniques, but certain fundamentals will never change unless the events themselves are changed. What we do intend, in the instances where this book departs from the fundamentals, is to show how techniques are adapted in a very individual way that has brought success to one of the authors, Peter Tancred.

The aim is to give an overview of each athletic throwing event, its history, plus a breakdown of the technique of each event including faults and corrective procedures as well as a clear indication of the training methods and procedures found by the authors to be of most value. We have been concerned to provide a fairly comprehensive overview of athletic throwing that will be of interest to competitive athletic throwers (novice and international alike); to multi-event athletes (decathletes and pentathletes, whose problems lie mainly in the area of throwing events); to coaches and teachers, who seek, not only technical information, but ideas about training for these events; and to the interested spectator who, having followed the fortunes of the 'big men' in athletics, now wishes to understand and appreciate the nature of the events themselves and the work that goes on behind the scenes of the Olympic and World Games.

The first chapter, Preparation Training, will concern itself with four main elements: strength, suppleness, speed and stamina, which we believe to be of fundamental importance both to the training and the coaching of successful athletes. We feel that it is possible that the lack of enthusiasm, on the part of our throwers in the past, for other concerns in training, apart from purely size and strength, may account for our lack of success in field events at major athletic competitions. It is by no means a coincidence that Peter, one of the smallest athletic throwers in the world, is one of Great Britain's best all-round throwers! It is his unique consideration of these, what should be, fundamentals that has enabled him to realize his potential. Thus, we hope that, being among the first to set them down in print for athletic throwers, we can provide the basis upon which athletes and coaches can proceed to greater success and reap the benefits of all the training that has concentrated on technique alone.

Chapters Two to Five will concern themselves, in turn, with each of the athletic throwing events: discus, shot, hammer, javelin. In each of these chapters the event will be broken down into its major parts so that the techniques may be examined, in simple and coachable terms, and possibly trained and emulated by the reader at his leisure. Each technique is illustrated by drawings with an additional photographic sequence illustrating Peter Tancred's particular style and interpretation.

In conclusion, we wish to point out that this book by no means exhausts all that possibly could be written about athletic throwing events. Its prime purpose is to promote interest and discussion as well as to provide further enjoyment for those people who maintain an interest in athletics. We hope that you will find this book interesting, useful and entertaining.

PETER TANCRED and CYRIL A. CARTER

I

Preparation Training

Preparation training refers to those activities performed by any athlete designed to enhance his performance at any chosen event. In the past such training has, at best, placed undue emphasis on one major quality (e.g. strength) thought vital to the event; at worst, it has been completely ignored in favour of total performance of the event itself. The continuing development of the sciences, in their application to the field of sports training, has led to a more systematic examination of the physical requirements necessary to achieve top performance. This in turn has led the athlete and his coach to organize training in a more systematic manner, so that results and achievements can be measured more scientifically. Unfortunately, the human factor in performance and the continuously variable psychological attitude of the athlete himself still allow for a great deal of variation in the degree of success attained by adopting any one system of preparation training.

Nevertheless, any athlete who has a serious intent to achieve the greatest degree of excellence possible in his chosen activity must consider the development of certain physical qualities that have been identified as having a vital influence on physical performance. These basic qualities have been termed the five S's; Strength, Suppleness, Speed, Stamina and Skill. In this book, it is our intention to separate skills training from the other qualities, because it is our belief that preparation training is more concerned with physiological properties which enhance the achievements of a skilled performance. In throwing one may be an extremely skilful performer and yet lack the other basic physical properties needed to achieve greater distance. Thus skills training concentrates more on the event itself, while preparation training concerns itself with developing the physical qualities to enhance a skilful performance.

11

Throwing events have generally been classified as 'power' events, compared with 'stamina' events (e.g. long distance running) or 'skill' events (e.g. archery). This classification has in the past led athletes to concentrate only upon developing that major quality by which their event has been categorized. Such classification presents a false picture to those young athletes who wish to aspire to success in throwing because such a classification, although seemingly specific, is only a generality. Just as some stamina events require strength, and strength events demand skill, so too does a throwing event require speed—as well as skill, stamina, strength and suppleness!

There are many training methods and systems from which the athlete can choose in order to develop the fundamental physical qualities. The majority have two things in common: first, they all apply the fundamental principles concerning the five S's (to a greater or lesser extent), second, they are all, at one time or another, sources of a great deal of argument. It is not the object of this book, nor is it our intention, to advocate any one particular system of training, nor any one particular exercise or series of exercises. Just as each athlete's psychological make-up is different, so too are his physical requirements, in terms of the degree of each quality already present, facilities and time available, the degree to which he can apply himself to work outside the event itself (i.e. relevance to the event), and general inherent physiology (size, sex and age). We intend to outline only the general principles involved and to detail only those exercises which we feel are specific to the event, and those which may be new to the athlete or which he has never considered. Thus we are concerned to detail the fundamental principles of preparation training and relate them to only a few of the various training techniques, which the athlete or coach may care to consider for inclusion into a 'specific' training programme designed for a 'unique' individual.

Each of the fundamental qualities is developed using the basic principles of training. Skill is developed by the consistent and constant repetition of an action, or series of actions, reducing the outlay of time, effort (physical and psychological) and energy in order to produce a desired result. Strength is increased by performing muscular work against a high load, or resistance. Suppleness is developed by performing 'work' at the extreme range of joint movement. Stamina is promoted by exercising under a low resistance over a long period of time in order to produce a durable condition of fatigue. Speed is enhanced (or achieved) by the performance of relatively high work loads over a short period of time.

Where possible, activities which are designed to develop these qualities should be closely related to the needs of the event itself. That is not to say that these activities must mirror the event itself, nor does it mean that the athlete develops, for example, *only* the range of movement (suppleness) required for his event. If, for example, the athlete trains with weights to mirror the delivery phase of shot putting, the result may often be a lack of speed, or a breakdown in skilled movement (timing), once the normal shot is resumed. Similarly, the development of only that range of movement which is required by shot putting, may encourage the athlete to work within the narrow confines of his own skill and movement, without regard to a view of himself as a complete athlete, which in turn may lead him to 'groove' a skill totally dependent upon the inherent physical qualities with which he first started training, or which develop naturally. If such were not the case then preparation training, in terms of supplementary exercises, would be unnecessary and the athlete could merely train at the event itself.

It must be remembered that preparation training is what its title implies, merely a procedure designed to prepare the athlete for performance at a specific event. Its purpose is to produce, or enhance, the necessary physical qualities which will ensure that the athlete is fit for a certain standard of performance at a particular sport and, as such, can never be regarded as a substitute for practice of the sport itself. Preparation training should at no time substitute for the performance of the event to the point where there is an obvious imbalance in any training programme, but neither should it be ignored as being merely gimmickry and dependent solely on the whims of the athlete or his coach.

Fitness is a general notion that implies very little unless one asks 'fit for what?'. In answering this question one considers certain aspects of the basic physical qualities necessary for performance at a specific sport or activity. Thus, fitness itself becomes specific and, in turn, influences the type of preparation activities undertaken by different sporting athletes. The degree and nature of preparation training are thus influenced by the type of event, and the needs of any one particular athlete—which allows for a great deal of variation! One unalterable fact about preparation training is that it is a continuous process. Unlike a piece of wood, which can be fashioned for a specific purpose for which it will always remain suited, a man can be trained towards a specific standard of performance, but is subject to decline and fluctuation unless he is continuously fashioned so as to take into account the complexities of his physiological and psychological make-up.

Unlike skill, which is developed slowly and never entirely disappears, the qualities of strength, suppleness, speed and stamina are developed comparatively quickly (at least initially), but rapidly disappear if training ceases for any reason. At first, and especially in the untrained person, preparation training produces rapid and easily measured results. For the highest performances, however, preparation training is a lengthy process, where results are not easily measured and performance is often more affected by mental attitude. It is the lack of a positive mental attitude towards preparation training which often results in a complete disregard for its benefits among many top athletes, who concentrate on the further development of their already well-defined skills. Such overemphasis often leads to an impasse so the athlete has to return to preparation training techniques in order to restore his physical fitness for the event. Therefore, and despite the inability to measure improvement at the highest level, the athlete should never disregard the continuous need for such training.

In the rest of this chapter we intend to outline the general principles involved in each of the fundamental physical aspects applicable to preparation training. But such a brief examination cannot be entirely comprehensive, nor have we the space in this book to provide complete details of the performance of all specific activities. Each section relates to a particular aspect of training, which is further outlined at the end of the subsequent chapters dealing with the particular throwing events.

Strength

For the human being, strength may be defined as the ability to use muscular tension in order to overcome resistance. Muscular tension refers to that activity in the muscle which causes it to become active and hypertrophic (i.e. simply to expand in size). Generally there are three main notions of strength: endurance strength, absolute strength (i.e. maximum strength) and explosive strength. In training the type of strength and the degree required can be achieved by the manipulation of three factors: the load or mass to be moved, the speed or acceleration by which it is moved, and the number of repetitions.

Endurance strength is possibly the first requirement of any young athlete aspiring to success in the throwing events. It is on the foundation of this basic type of strength that the qualities of maximum strength and power are to be developed. This type of strength is fostered by the movement of loads (weights) approximately 75 per cent of the maximum ability of the individual, and over a number of repetitions. Thus, if the individual can, for example, bench-press 100 kg only once (maximum strength in this exercise), then he will reduce the weight to approximately 70 kg and attempt to perform the same exercise a number of times consecutively (e.g. 8). As he finds the performance of a set number of repetitions becoming progressively easier, he may then gradually begin to increase the weight to be moved. In this manner muscular efficiency is improved and, provided an all-round weight training routine is used, both local and general endurance is improved.

Absolute strength is any one individual's maximum capacity to manipulate (or lift) a heavy load only once. Thus, for example, if in bench-press the athlete can perform only one repetition at 100 kg weight and cannot repeat this movement consecutively, this would be an indication of his absolute strength at this exercise. Absolute strength is fostered by the use of weights in order to overload the muscles in an attempt to make them perform work at maximum intensity over a minimum of repetitions. There are several methods from which the athlete may choose in order to develop maximum strength in any particular exercise using weights. Possibly the most popular method is to use the system of 'progressive overload'. For this method the athlete must first find out what his initial maximum performance is at present. From this he would deduct between 5 and 10 kg (depending on the exercise), which he would perform twice, and with further deductions to perform 4 times, 6 times, and 8 times. Thus, for example, progressive overload on bench-press would be performed as follows:

MAXIMUM WEIGHT (lift once)   —   100 kg
MINUS 5 kg (lift 2 times)   —   95 kg

MINUS 10 kg (lift 4 times)	—	90 kg
MINUS 15 kg (lift 6 times)	—	85 kg
MINUS 20 kg (lift 8 times)	—	80 kg

starting with the lightest weight (80 kg) and maximum number of repetitions (8) and working upward until the maximum weight is reached. As performance becomes progressively easier (or maximum strength has been found to increase) the weights at each stage are slightly increased, in order to ensure overload of the muscles involved.

Explosive strength is the type of strength required by the athletic thrower and should not be confused with maximum strength. Explosive strength or power, refers to that ability to move the optimum amount of weight at speed. It is extremely difficult to measure the optimum strength of an athlete, except in terms of his performance at a particular throwing event itself, whereas maximum strength simply involves moving the maximum amount of weight (regardless of speed). Nevertheless, power may be developed by selecting those weight-lifting exercises or activities which require fast co-ordination and which should be as specific to the event as possible. Such exercises should be performed with weights slightly below the athlete's maximum, and the object should be to perform each exercise at maximum speed over several repetitions. For the experienced athlete an alternative method of developing power is increasing or reducing the weight of the implement he will use in practice. Reducing the weight may help the athlete to speed up and produce a faster co-ordination within his technique. Increasing the weight will force the athlete to work harder in applying his power to the implement. It is inadvisable to deviate from the competition weight of the implement by more than ± 1 kg (in the case of shot and discus), ± 2 kg (in the case of hammer), and ± 1 kg in simulating the javelin technique by use of a heavy ball. Care should be taken to ensure that such practices do not have an adverse effect upon technique, therefore the competition weight implement should be returned to as quickly as possible.

A further quality of strength which we wish to outline is that of 'strength-in-extension'. Quite simply this type of strength is similar to the gymnast's ability to hold positions and move weight at the extreme range of his reach. If one examines the delivery phase of each of the throwing events, one can easily see that the athlete is called upon to apply his power over his maximum range of movement (this being the essence of athletic throwing). The majority of training with weights does not in itself provide for increases in such strength; although some exercises can be devised which will be effective to a certain extent. Our preference is for a method which utilizes a suitable strong length of rubber tubing (e.g. an inner tube from either a bicycle or car, with the valve cut out and cut into strips if necessary).

In athletic throwing we are concerned for the strengthening of the shoulders, arms, upper back, and chest in order that the throwing arm can apply its strength throughout its greatest range. In order to develop co-ordinated strength-in-extension it is necessary for the athlete to perform a series of exercises involving the complete range of movement of both arms. The following illustrations show the best method of training for this type of strength:

1. Deltoids (front shoulder)

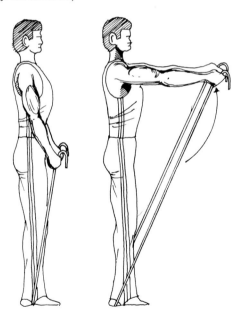

2. Trapezii and Deltoids (shoulder and neck)

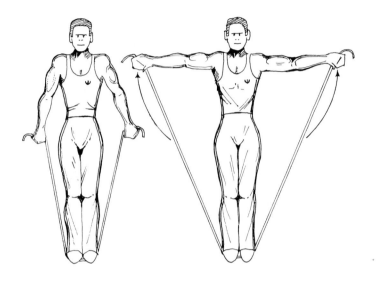

3. Deltoids (rear shoulder and upper back)

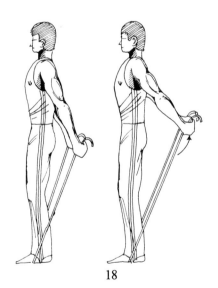

4. *Latissimus Dorsi and Pectorals (side and front chest)*

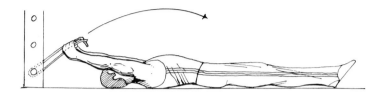

5. *Lats (side chest)*

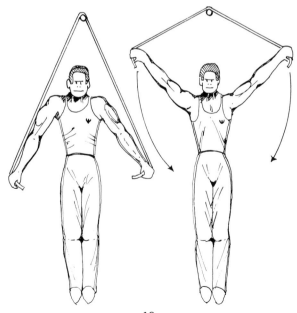

Additionally, rubber tubing can be used in a simulation of the throwing action by attaching it to a fixture at a suitable height behind the athlete so he performs his action while simultaneously holding on to a suitable length of tubing.

A word of warning: muscles have to be educated into working in extension, so at first do not try to be too ambitious—after several weeks' training with these exercises you can approach the task much more seriously.

Suppling

In this section we are concerned to avoid any confusion between suppling and 'mobility exercising'. In our opinion many of the activities performed under the title of mobility exercising are often amusing and sometimes horrifying. Many athletes appear to be confused as to their aim in using such exercises and how best to achieve it. Further, it appears that the title mobility exercising has contributed much to that confusion and often allowed for the performance of exercises which were almost useless and sometimes downright dangerous. The time has come when these practices should be re-examined.

Mobility itself refers to the ability to move, to the fact that something is not fixed, and that such movement can be performed voluntarily (when dealing with a healthy human body). Exercise refers to the practice of exercising muscles etc. for health's sake, also moving voluntarily. The expression mobility exercising, because it carries no proper indication of range of movement, would thus appear to mean 'moving movement' and, as such, is meaningless.

That is not to say that mobility exercising has no meaning at all; unfortunately it has, but its meaning depends entirely upon the associations it has for the person using it, and the qualities such 'exercising' brings about lie also within the mind of the user and, often, exploiter. What exactly are we, or should we, be aiming at when we talk about 'mobility'?

Clearly, it is not just the ability to move freely, for if we couldn't, we should be more inclined to seek the services of a doctor, or mortician! In our concern for what are termed the five S's: Skill, Speed, Stamina, Strength and Suppleness it would seem to be the last quality, supple-

20

ness, for which we should have a major concern. Suppleness refers to the qualities of bending, pliancy and flexibility, a range of movement to be achieved at our joints. Suppling would thus refer directly to exercises specifically designed to promote or increase the *range* of movement and not just movement alone. It seems to us this is what people mean when they talk about mobility exercising, and therefore they should use the correct term suppling in order to exclude those exercises which do little or nothing of the sort.

Suppling is often confused with contortion, which means to twist and distort, and it is not our intention to advocate exercises other than those which promote the more natural movements of the limbs. Nor is it our intention to suggest that athletes should be capable of some of the movements performed by competitive gymnasts although, in some instances, this would not necessarily be a bad thing.

Our intention is to show that suppling is a far more structured and scientific process than is generally imagined, that it is based on sound principles of safety and effectiveness, and that suppleness is not merely a quality that only the talented few retain from birth. It is our hope that the myth of mobility exercising can be exploded to expose its proper intentions and to eliminate any bad, or ineffective, practices.

GENERAL PRINCIPLES

The general principles of suppling may be observed in the practice of positions in some forms of yoga, ballet and gymnastics where the object is to achieve a series of positions which will promote the natural range of movements of both the hip and shoulder girdle, so the more explosive elements of movement can be performed at the extremes of range, with little strain and with minimal risk of injury to muscles and joints.

There are many different forms of suppling, but the method which we advocate for all athletic throwers is what may be called passive suppling (as opposed to active). The main principle governing this is that the athlete should never use his own muscular strength to attempt to *force* a joint beyond its natural range. We have seen athletes bouncing their trunks up and down while sitting in a hurdling position; this is to some extent ineffective and possibly dangerous. The natural reaction of a trained muscle when encountering a sudden movement is to tighten up and take the majority of strain in a natural attempt to prevent injury to the joint. This natural reaction counters the effort of stretching and lengthening (suppling) the muscle and ligaments and often causes small tears (not the weeping variety) in the muscle itself. Often these small injuries pass unnoticed until the point when enough scar tissue is built up to cause discomfort, stiffness and often pain. Athletes should remember that injured muscle fibres are not replaced in the same way that skin heals and that scar tissue can often only be removed by surgery, sometimes unsuccessfully.

In all exercises for suppling the emphasis is on relaxation of the limb to be worked upon. Therefore, whatever position is being practised, the athlete must attempt to go to the extremes of his range and stay relaxed in that position for a period of time. It is the amount of times one adopts such positions, together with the length of time spent in them, which determine just how supple one is likely to get and how quickly. The only effort required is the effort involved in relaxing (and in modern-day man that *is* an effort) and, to some extent, the effort involved in enduring a suppling programme!

Suppling is an all-round process. This means that it is of little use suppling in one direction without spending an equal amount of time suppling in the naturally opposite direction. For example, if one requires suppleness in the hamstrings for the leading leg action in hurdling, one must also supple the quadriceps (the opposite direction) on the same leg. All attempts to supple in one direction are to some extent countered by the stiffness and strength of muscles that are not being supplied. This is on the principle that for every movement there is a muscle which acts as a prime mover and another which acts as an antagonist. This aids strong and stable movement. Suppling the antagonist only is thus countered by the tension and stiffness of the prime mover (and vice versa), therefore both are to be supplied.

To a certain extent any athlete or coach should have some firm knowledge (not just old wives' tales) of physiology and anatomy. Although the above may be insufficient to cover *all* the principles of suppling (as far as we are concerned) it is enough technical detail for the moment. The question most athletes and coaches ask is: 'What can we actually do?'

BASIC SUPPLING
The following is a basic programme which can be practised by the individual alone (as opposed to pairs or assisted suppling). Often these exercises substitute as a safe and effective warm-up for both training

and competition for all athletes, whether track or field. Any times and numbers which we have applied may be regarded purely as a guide and may be expanded at the discretion of the athlete or his coach. For the best results these exercises should be performed as often as possible (at least once a day and preferably prior to training and in the sequence given).

HIP GIRDLE

Leg swinging: this serves to prepare the hip joint for the actual suppling which is to follow. To a great extent it promotes suppleness and it is the only activity, apart from arm swinging, in which the athlete will use his own muscles for movement. There are three natural directions in which the hip should be suppled and swung: forward, backward and sideways. All swinging movements are performed in an upright position, ensuring that the leg which is not swinging remains at all times with the heel firmly in contact with the ground. It is desirable that a wall-bar, or other fixture at about waist height, is held for extra balance.

Forward: stand sideways to the wall and swing the outside leg upward towards the chest. Backward: stand at arm's length facing the wall (or fixture to be held) and swing each leg from a 'hurdle-step' position backward, while bending forward slightly at the waist. Sideways: stand in the same position as for 'backward', take the swinging

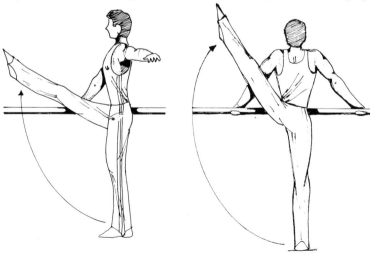

leg across the body slightly and swing it upward and to the side (not turning the hips). It is important to note that in all movements the swinging leg must be kept perfectly straight and the head should be held up while the supporting leg remains both straight and still. Perform each exercise at least 10 times for each leg.

Hamstrings (back of the thigh): sit either in a hurdle position, or with both legs held together and straight, and attempt to lower your stomach on to your thighs. The back must be kept straight and head up throughout. Lower as much as possible and hold for thirty seconds, in the case of hurdle position, on each leg. Perform at least three times.

Quadriceps (front of the thigh): kneel down on one leg at full stretch. The bent, front leg should form an angle greater than 90 degrees so that it does not over-support. The stretched back leg should form a bow, with the toes pointed. The trunk and head should be upright or leaning slightly backward. Gravity, and the weight of your own body, will do the rest. Hold for 30 seconds and perform at least twice on each leg.

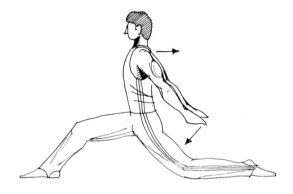

Hamstrings/Quadriceps: for those who have achieved a good degree of suppleness, practise splits. Straighten both legs, forward and backward, and lower body gently, as far as possible. Keep the trunk and head upright by holding on to a suitable fixture. Hold for 10 seconds each way and repeat twice.

Sideways at the hip: stand square facing a bar or other surface at waist height. Raise one leg and place it on the bar. Keeping the trunk upright, hips square to the wall and with both legs straight, slide the supported leg outward gently as far as possible. Hold for 20 seconds and repeat twice for each leg.

Box splits: stand square to a wall bar as before and slide both legs out sideways until the maximum range is reached. Keep both legs straight, hips forward and square, trunk and head upright. Hold for 20 seconds and repeat twice.

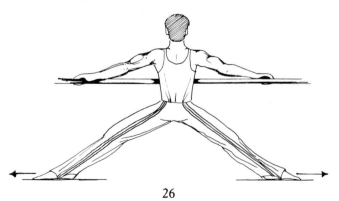

SHOULDER GIRDLE

Arm swinging: most athletes are familiar with arm-circling movements and these are excellent as a preliminary to actual suppling. Care should be taken to ensure that the arms perform the widest circles possible, touching the ears and the sides while maintaining straight arms.

Basically we are concerned to supple the arms in two directions: one, when the arms are held straight backward over the head; two, when the arms are taken from a position at the side, backward and upward to the rear.

Backward above the head: using a wall bar at waist height, take a grip with the hands at about shoulder width apart and bend forward at the waist so that your arms and back form a straight line. Keeping the arms straight (but relaxed) bend hard at the waist until the maximum shoulder range is reached. The coach may assist this movement by placing some of his weight on the athlete's shoulders with his hands. Hold for 30 seconds and repeat 3 times.

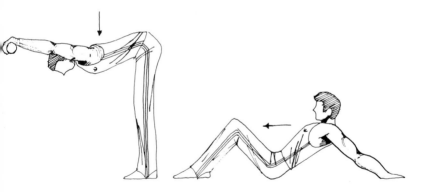

Upward behind the back: sit on the floor with your arms stretched out behind you, the hands as close together as possible. Slide forward, holding the head up, until the maximum range is reached. Maintain for 30 seconds and repeat 3 times.

This by no means exhausts the possible types or number of suppling exercises which can safely be performed. Whatever other activity you discover under the term suppling, remember that it is a long and slow process (often painful—but not injurious) where the emphasis is on relaxation NOT on activity. If you encounter any *sudden* or *sharp* pain, stop immediately! Take your time and persevere for, just as the results are slow, so too are they certain AND SAFE!

Speed

Speed may be defined as the ability of the nervous system to effect muscular movement in order to perform any action or series of actions at a certain velocity. In athletic throwing the intention is simply to apply the maximum degree of force over the greatest distance and with the greatest amount of speed. Given this, it appears that speed must be a vital factor to be considered in any form of preparation training. However, physiological research has suggested that the maximum speed of muscular contraction in any one individual is already determined at birth. From this it would appear that training may have very little effect upon increasing the maximum speed in any individual's performance. This, however, is not strictly true because, when dealing with such skills as throwing, we are talking of a complex series of co-ordinated movements that are designed to build up in such a manner that speed is only vital in the final phase (i.e. delivery) of each technique.

In throwing events consistency, accuracy, and fluidity in the application of power are often more vital than the achievement of maximum speed upon delivery. If accuracy and fluidity are sacrificed in favour of pure speed, the result is often an incorrect, or poor, performance. This an important factor to bear in mind, especially in the early stages of learning. During these early stages the practice of any skilled movement should be performed at much less than maximum speed, in order to foster a higher degree of accuracy. This is based on the principle that it is often more difficult to correct fast but inaccurate movements than it is to speed up accurate movements. Therefore, the aim of any athletic thrower should be to apply the maximum degree of force over the greatest distance with the greatest amount of speed, but with the perfection of movement in the desired skill.

All else being equal, and with the condition of skill having been satisfied, speed will then have an important part to play in the achievement of success in the throwing events. In order better to realize the athlete's potential of maximum speed he needs to develop quick responses, the ability to accelerate smoothly and proficiently, and the ability to maintain speed under physical pressure. To a certain extent practice of the event itself, combined with strength training and suppling, will do much to develop such speed. Other activities may, however, aid in developing the athlete's ability to respond quickly and promote speed endurance. Such activities are detailed in the relevant section of each of the following chapters.

Stamina

Stamina quite simply refers to the power of endurance and may be defined as the ability to perform a certain degree of work over a long period of time, without any deterioriation in the quality of performance. In the majority of physical activities we are concerned with two types of endurance: strength-endurance and speed-endurance. Strength-endurance may be fostered by following the principle of strength training outlined above, while speed-endurance (specific to the event) is fostered by the repetitive performances involved in technique training. In the well-trained and experienced athlete, the factor of endurance has very little effect upon his performance in competition, purely because there is an adequate amount of recovery time between each separate performance of the technique.

General endurance is, however, an important factor for any athlete to consider, especially during the out-of-season and the early pre-season period of training. In this context, such stamina training should be regarded as an important part of the conditioning phase that prepares the athlete for the rigours of the more intense forms of technique and strength training that will follow.

Programmed Training

Any training programme, if it is to be successful, must be constructed in such a way that it takes into account the specific needs of the individual and the demands of the event itself. If it is properly constructed, it will take more account of remedying his weaknesses

29

rather than promoting his strengths. No training programme can remain static and should be subject to constant change and addition in order to suit constantly changing physiological conditions and practical demands.

Although, for convenience, we generally split the year into several main parts (i.e. out of season, pre-season, and competitive season), and choose to place greater emphasis on certain types of training in each of the different parts, this is merely a guide and takes no account of the individual demands of any one particular athlete. It may be that, for reasons of injury (or otherwise), heavy strength-training may have to be resumed during some part of the competitive season. What we have tried to do is indicate what we feel is the most desirable period for each type of training.

Individuals and their circumstances are unique. It follows, then, that any given training programme must by necessity, also be unique. In order for the athlete or his coach to take into account this uniqueness, it is vital that a training diary should be kept religiously up to date. This diary should record all relevant aspects of the athlete's training: types of exercise, numbers of repetitions, amount of weight used in strength training, success or otherwise in technique training—as well as notes on technical performance (especially changes and their effect), and even some diagnosis of the reasons for success or failure, and any advice given by coaches and other performers, in fact everything that may be relevant to the achievement of a highly skilled physical performance (even diet, changes in habit or other factors which may affect motivation). Above all, beware the coach and even other performers who advocate one particular system of training (including fads) for *all* competitors, irrespective of any sense of uniqueness.

Note: in the following chapters we have outlined only those exercises which we feel are specific to the event and which have provided success for one of the authors in athletic throwing.

II

Discus

History of the Event

Discus throwing is unique in that it is one of the oldest, by tradition, of all the athletic throwing events. Its origins are firmly rooted historically in activities practised by ancient Greek cultures, as shown by the sculpture *Discobolus* by Myron. It is one of the few athletic events that can be recognized as being practised in both the ancient and modern Olympic Games.

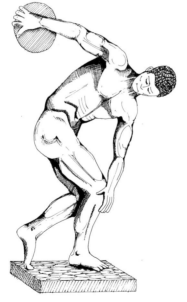

As can be seen from the *Discobolus*, the Greek style of throwing was performed from a raised pedestal (balbis), which placed severe limitations upon the athlete. As well as this restriction upon technique, the greater weight and diameter of the discus itself compared with today's implement prevented throwers from attaining distances greater than 100 ft (30.5 m) compared with modern throws of 200 ft (61 m) plus. Until 1896 all competitions required that the discus be thrown 'Greek style', but in that year, a 7 ft (2.13 m) circle was introduced which allowed throwers to invent and adopt the so-called 'free style' in which competitors could move across the circle before delivering the throw. In 1910, the IAAF (International Amateur Athletic Federation) adopted a circle measuring 2.5 m (8 ft 2½ in), which remains to this day. Such innovations led to an increase in the distances possible for the discus thrower. Further advancement in this event can be attributed to such things as conversion from grass to concrete circles and improved footwear enabling better balance, timing and manoeuvrability leading to improved performances and better techniques.

The discus itself has become more precisioned. Scientific attention was turned to the manufacturing of an implement that had greater aerodynamic qualities which would aid its flight and add precious distance to the achievements of the competent athlete. The first of these technically improved implements was the French 'Obol'. With most of the weight being situated around the rim, the discus was made to spin longer, which helped to stabilize its gyroscopic action. Experiments by J. A. Taylor in the 1930s revealed that such a design allows the discus to spin at over 300 r.p.m., at average speed, which disturbs the air in such a way as to produce a 'lifting' current, known as a 'magnus effect', thus enabling the athlete to throw for even greater distance.

More significant changes have occurred in the athletes themselves. The availability of greater leisure time with the resulting increase in available facilities has allowed athletes to become more dedicated, paying more scientific attention to phasing training programmes and to such things as diet. Greater thought is given to the content of training schedules, with more emphasis on specific exercises that are directly applicable to, and often simulate, the event. Consequently modern athletes are much stronger and fitter than their predecessors and are more prone to analysing, experimenting and modifying their technique. Communication between athletes about training methods and technical information have served to breathe greater interest and enthusiasm into the event.

Athletes now concern themselves with questions of style and technique, the most popular being to contrast American methods with those used mainly by the Eastern Europeans. The East Germans, in particular, prefer a more rotational action of throwing, which is facilitated by swinging the right leg away from the left with a high 'pick-up' of the knee and 'clipping-in' the right foot at the point of landing in the middle of the circle. One of the main exponents of this technique is Wolfgang Schmidt (E Germany).

In contrast to this, the American style of throwing differs in their preference to maintain a more linear approach. This is brought about by a similar high 'pick-up' of the right leg, but the knee is kept closer to the left leg during the drive across the circle. This is loosely termed 'the running rotational style'—resembling the action of a sprinter. The form of the delivery differs from that of Eastern Europeans in that, because they prefer a 'hinged' locked left leg at this point, the Americans favour a more active reverse, which looks to a casual observer almost like a premature jump. For the moment it is enough to know that such technical controversy exists and further details may be found later in this chapter, where we shall be more concerned with technique.

Although it is the aim of the discus thrower to achieve the greatest distances possible, such improvements that have been made have resulted in the paradoxical situation that the throwing area is becoming so long that it may not be possible to contain it within the in-field of a running track for much longer. With throws in excess of 220 ft (approximately 67 m) there is an increasing danger to track athletes competing at the same time. It would seem, therefore, that we must eventually take a step backwards to the days of ancient Greece by increasing the weight of the discus; although such an increase may not make it as large, it will certainly have a radical effect upon the distances achievable in world performance. It could also reinforce the fact that the highest achievements in this event will remain the province of the largest and the strongest of athletes.

SAFETY ASPECTS
Because the discus is potentially a dangerous event, strict adherence to safety rules must be observed and applied at all times. Many accidents are often caused through carelessness, such as throwing the implement back towards the circle on retrieving it.
1. In competition, do not throw until you have been told to do so.

2. During the preparatory stages of warming-up, it is advisable not to throw in any direction apart from the circle provided, and then only throw in that set direction.

3. Always make sure that the landing area is clear before commencing the throw.

4. Never enter the throwing area to retrieve a discus while the circle is still in use.

Note. The throwing area should be roped off, and the discus circle should, ideally, be enclosed with a safety net. Much more could be said about safety, but it is our hope that common sense will take over after acknowledging these simple rules.

Breakdown of the Event

In this section, we have broken the event down into its component parts in order that the fundamental aspects of technique can be more easily examined. Having done so, we should warn the athlete and the coach of the need to ensure that the final, complete technique should be fluid and not merely a make-up of these parts. Some of these fundamental aspects may be adapted according to the style and size of the athlete, most of them not. Both coaches and athletes should become fully aware of when changes are due to 'improved' style, and of when they are merely FAULTS!

Note: although we have described the technique for a right-handed thrower, a reversal of all directions will result in a left-handed technique.

THE HOLD

It is important to note that the discus is not gripped in any way. The discus is held in such a way that it rests flat upon the palm of the up-turned, throwing hand with the finger-tips spread evenly around its rim, merely to 'cradle' it. If the hand was reversed in this position then the discus would fall to the ground. The thumb merely rests against the surface of the discus, with the whole hand being relaxed and the wrist kept straight. Apart from the fact that the thumb may regulate the angle of flight upon release (as we shall see later) at this point it is merely supportive, acting as a stabilizer rather than a grasping member.

34

Although there is an obvious tendency to grip the discus, rest assured that the centrifugal force caused by the preliminary swings and the turn across the circle, will cause the discus to press against the finger-tips, thus preventing it from falling from the hand. If, however, the finger-tips are not placed firmly against the rim, or if at any point the arm stops swinging, then gravity will take over and the discus will fall from the hand.

THE STANCE

The stance refers to the starting position taken up prior to commencing the throw and will obviously vary slightly according to the size and style of the athlete. Essentially, the stance should be a relaxed position to ensure concentration prior to starting the technique. An appropriate and functional position will be achieved if the athlete positions his feet slightly wider than shoulder width apart, at the rear of the circle and opposite to the direction of the desired throw.

The feet should straddle an imaginary line running directly across the circle, from the back towards the direction of the throw (from 6 to 12 o'clock), ensuring that the left heel will clear the protruding rim during the pivoting movement which is to follow. The knees should be slightly flexed, as if commencing to sit on a high chair, with the hips kept forward, back straight and head held erect. Although the degree of knee bend may, in some part, depend upon the leg strength of the athlete, the body weight should be balanced in this position to ensure stability and manoeuvrability within the circle.

35

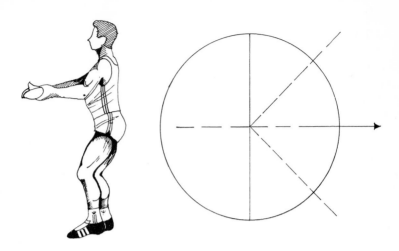

PRELIMINARY SWING

The preliminary swing refers to the movement which sets the athlete up in the correct position immediately prior to commencing the turn across the circle. Many athletes prefer to take several preliminary swings before commencing to throw, but it is our opinion that this is usually as a result of inadequate concentration and practice of this part of the technique. Although this may seem a harsh comment, it is our experience that some throwers perform every preliminary swing correctly (being balanced, etc.) except the one which immediately precedes the throw, which is usually performed too strongly thus leading to faults of balance and technique. Having said this, however, we can add that such swings may aid the athlete in preparing and concentrating which, if the final swing is *always* correctly performed, may be of value. But, it should be noted that where extra performance is added then, correspondingly, there are extra areas in which mistakes can occur. In this section we are concerned only with that swing which occurs immediately before the execution of the actual throwing technique.

The function of the preliminary swing is to set the athlete up in a correct position with the right, throwing arm out and to the rear of the body, in order to create a position where potential force can be generated that can be enhanced and exploited later in the technique. This potential force is called 'torque' and refers to the force created by

36

twisting one end of an object against its fixed, other end (in this case, the body).

After a gentle swing to the left of the body the straight right arm swings to the right and behind the athlete, while the left arm curls loosely up and across the chest to relieve excess tension. While performing this movement, the lower part of the body is 'locked' and held relatively static, with its weight shifted to 'sit' over the right heel. Although this movement should be performed strongly, it should not be excessive, or this may lead to a false position due to an over-reaction (rebound) of the body in which the arm catches up, and, subsequently, to loss of torque. Throughout this movement, the right foot should remain firmly in contact with the ground while the left may turn slightly on to the toe. Care should be taken to ensure that the athlete's weight is well balanced over the right heel, that the shoulders are square and body virtually upright (seat kept well in), and that the left knee does not bend too much and close towards the right. It should be stressed that any faults occurring at this stage will, almost automatically, result in other major faults in the rest of the technique—much of an athlete's, and coach's, time can be wasted by correcting these major faults and failing to pay enough attention to the preliminary swing. All being well, the athlete should now be in the correct position to commence the next part of the technique.

THE SET-UP

This phase is concerned with the transition between the point where the athlete has completed the preliminary swing to the position where he is ready to commence his drive across the circle, involving a rotation to the point where the athlete (still at the back of the circle) can see the throwing area.

At this point in the preliminary swing, where the shoulders have achieved their greatest rotation, the athlete now begins to pivot on the ball of his left foot, towards the direction of the throw. This pivoting motion resembles the stubbing-out of a cigarette (always assuming that an athlete has had only second-hand experience of this habit!). At the same time, the athlete should quickly, and strongly, turn the left shoulder, arm and head in the direction of the throw, so that the left side of the body (still balanced) attempts to run strongly away from the throwing arm and shoulder. Thus the athlete pivots on his left foot, with the knee still flexed and turning away from the right, just as his weight is transferring from his right heel on to the ball of his left foot. The result should be that the left side of the athlete will lead into the throw by running away from the right.

It is vitally important to note that the athlete's body weight should pass around and over the left foot, and never outside it nor in between the legs. If the weight passes outside the left foot, it will mean that the thrower will adopt a piked (bent forward) position, causing him to under rotate at the rear of the circle. If his weight passes in a direction

38

between his legs, this will result in the athlete 'falling' across the circle and effectively prevent him from using his right 'driving' leg efficiently.

Having previously been solidly fixed to the ground, the right foot comes off the ground at the point where the athlete's weight is firmly over his left foot. This right leg moves out and around the left to a position where it is ready to be swung and kicked into the drive across the circle. Although this whole movement should be performed strongly, its speed should be relatively gradual and progressive, rather than continuous and sudden.

THE DRIVE

The athlete should now be poised in a sprinting position, facing the direction of the throw. At this point, the athlete attempts to swing and kick his right leg into the centre of the circle (increasing his rotation) and, just as the right leg overtakes the left, the left foot pushes off to enhance the sprinting action (increasing linear drive).

This is made possible by not thinking in terms of turning away from the right arm. On the contrary, the athlete must attempt to hold the left foot at a position pointing slightly left of centre of the circle (11 o'clock), while maintaining a focal point in the same direction. At this point, the athlete commences his drive by kicking strongly with his right leg towards the centre of the circle, while pushing off vigorously with the left foot at the point when the right leg overtakes it. This should ensure that the athlete is driving towards the direction of the desired throw. During this driving phase the athlete should attempt to run against his outstretched left arm, which is pointing towards the front of the circle.

Ensuring that the driving right leg is kept close to the ground, the athlete then attempts to 'clip' his right foot inwards, immediately prior to it striking the centre of the circle. This will mean that the right foot, on landing, will be facing a position just left of centre of the back of the circle (a 190-degree turn). The effect of this important movement is to produce a considerable amount of rotation which will enhance the torque set up in the preliminary swing. The athlete must attempt to clip the foot in a movement well in excess of 180 degrees (i.e. with the toe of the right foot facing the rear of the circle); anything less will result in loss of torque, and a final position at the delivery stage where the right hip is unable to explode into the throw (called 'blocking'). It is also essential that balance is maintained throughout this part of the technique, therefore practice of this phase is essential.

If this stage is performed correctly, the result should be a fast, balletic movement which, although placing tremendous demands upon concentration and confidence, will result in a more efficient and successful performance.

Having clipped the right leg into a position at the centre of the circle, the left foot should be picked up, passing close to the right knee, and kicked back behind the athlete to land almost simultaneously in a position at the front of the circle. If this left foot lands to the left of centre, at the front, the athlete is landing 'in the bucket', giving instability and an early and shallow hip drive. If it lands to the right of centre, then the athlete will block on delivery. Therefore, it is essential that the left foot lands in the centre of the front of the circle in a position where the toe is in line with the heel of the right foot.

During the drive, the athlete will run against his left arm which, helped by the clipping action, will automatically wrap lightly against his chest, similar to the action of a ballet dancer performing a pirouette. One important point to remember is that the left leg, in its kick to the front of the circle, should not be taken out wide as this will lead to overbalancing. The athlete should attempt to clap the inside of his knees together at this point in order to avoid that tendency.

The athlete should now be in a position to commence the 'delivery' phase, with the athlete looking towards the right and rear of the circle, shoulders square, the right leg in the centre of the circle, and the left

leg placed at the front, with the throwing arm still remaining fully behind the rotation of the body. It is important to note that the feet should not be too close together or this will result in throwing off the back (right) leg, possible scooping of the discus, premature jumping and even fouling the circle. Furthermore, insufficient kneebend will cause a loss of leg drive, while too much will result in the discus leaving the hand before the legs have been straightened; this is a matter for each individual to sort out.

THE DELIVERY

The final pull should be initiated as soon as the left foot is planted at the front of the circle, immediately following the drive across the circle. The athlete should, at this stage, avoid the temptation to drop either shoulder, or to turn the head in the direction of the throw, before the legs and hips have done their work.

Our preference is to favour a two-legged drive into the delivery phase and this is initiated by turning the right foot and knee towards the direction of the throw. Thus, the athlete attempts to pivot the right knee against the left until the hips are almost square on to the direction of the throw, both legs still remaining flexed. At this point, the left foot straightens vigorously, causing the right leg to pivot and push against the resisting left leg, which results in the athlete having to rise on the balls of both feet. This, in turn, gives him maximum range on final delivery. In this style of delivery, as with any other style, it should be stressed that only the left foot gives the elevation to the discus, and not the right.

If the action so far has been carried out fluently, the right trailing arm should come into play by following the right hip, chest and shoulder into the direction of the throw. It is important to stress that the sequence of events should be legs, right hip, chest, shoulder, followed smoothly by the right, throwing arm. As the throwing arm is unleashed across the face of the athlete, his head should be held high and facing the direction of the throw. It should be remembered that the head is a rudder—looking down will, in effect, cause the discus to be thrown downward. Therefore, during the driving action with the legs, the head, which was previously looking to the rear of the circle, now looks round and up, causing the body to arch slightly, like a bow primed for shooting.

The desired angle of release and the plane of the discus during its

41

flight depend, in some part, upon the speed of the prevailing wind. With little or no wind, the angle of release and plane of the discus should be around 30 degrees from the horizontal. The angle of release is assisted by the amount of pressure the thumb and fingers exert at the point when the discus leaves the hand, decreasing the pressure of the forefinger, increasing the pressure of the little finger, plus exerting pressure on the top of the discus with the thumb, resulting in a raising of the front of the discus and, therefore, an increase in the angle of release. It should be stressed that, during the intitial learning stages, the throwing hand should always be held parallel to the ground (palm downwards), in order to minimize the likelihood of an incorrect angle of flight on release.

Throughout this phase of the throw, the athlete should ensure that the right leg drives the direction of the throw before the left, in order to maintain the pull on the discus and prevent a catching up of the right, throwing arm. If the right knee goes higher than the left, before the hips are facing the direction of the throw, the lifting will occur too early, forcing the athlete to fall over his left foot and causing the discus to be released too early. If, on the other hand, the right knee drops towards the left, then an over-arching of the back will occur, resulting in the discus being scooped up from the right hip.

The athlete should now be in a position at the front of the circle, with the discus having just left the hand. The throwing arm should be pointing the discus away with the head and eyes looking up into the direction of the throw. The left foot will be braced at the front of the circle with the right foot behind and slightly to the right. The whole body should be stretching into the throw with the feet just about to leave the ground after the legs have completed all their work. The problem now is to remain in the circle and prevent a foul.

THE REVERSE

Although the reverse should be as automatic as possible and is a vital part of this technique, overemphasis can result in the athlete's being so inhibited that he may resist attempting to achieve maximum velocity in the delivery phase. On the other hand, too little emphasis can result in continuous fouling of the circle in competitions, which is possibly more disastrous. Therefore, the athlete must balance these two dangers in such a way that enough attention and practising are applied to ensure that an automatic, safe and uninhibited technique is achieved.

Many throwers prefer a scissor-like technique to prevent fouling the circle. This is achieved by allowing both legs to leave the ground immediately on release of the discus and switching the right leg with the left leg in a fast exchange of positions. An immediate bend of the right leg, coupled with a raising of the left leg, results in a lowering of the athlete's centre of gravity, effectively reducing forward momentum and bringing the athlete to a halt (an active reverse).

43

Our preference is for the novice athlete to remain with both legs on the ground, so as to learn to use his legs more efficiently on delivery. Later on he may prefer to adopt the active reverse, or even adapt his own method of restraint, suitable to his own technique. All being well, the athlete should now have completed his throw, kept within the circle, and be awaiting the results of his efforts.

1

2

3

4

5

6

7

8

Faults and Corrective Procedures

In this section we shall attempt to examine those faults most commonly experienced by young, inexperienced throwers. Any list of faults could be endless, so we have selected only those major faults which we have observed in the training and throwing of young athletes.

Correction of these faults is difficult for the athlete alone and usually requires the trained eye of a good coach in order to achieve success quickly and effectively. Although we have written this section primarily for coaches, it is useful for the athlete to take good note so he can better evaluate his own technique and better appreciate any advice his coach might give.

1. Over-rotation in the rear half of the circle: This fault occurs in the transition between the set-up and the drive across the circle. What usually happens is that the athlete attempts to spin on his left foot in the set-up and, instead of driving directly across the circle in a sprinting action, he is forced to 'windmill' his way to the throwing position. The result is a total loss of balance, co-ordination and power in the throw. Usually his throwing becomes totally unpredictable because of the many variations in body position resulting at the front of the circle and a lot of time is often wasted in trying to correct them. This fault is often caused by a failure of the athlete to achieve the correct position in the set-up, in looking, and subsequently driving, directly to the front of the circle, by pushing off with the left foot and maintaining his linear direction until the right leg has clipped in to land in the centre.

To correct this fault the athlete must ensure that his left foot becomes more active in pushing off when attempting the drive across the circle; that the drive is only towards the direction of the throw (i.e. directly towards the front of the circle), and that the left leg is fully extended in completing its pushing action. This latter may be observed by the coach standing in a suitable position at the side of the circle.

A suitable progressive practice is to start the drive with the right leg standing outside the circle, so that the athlete can commence the drive without first turning. Gradually the right leg can be positioned at various points to the desired starting point until the full turn and drive are achieved successfully.

2. Falling across the rear half of the circle: This fault also occurs in the transition between the set-up and the drive across the circle. What usually happens is that the athlete attempts to drive across the circle prematurely, before he is facing the direction of the throw. The result is that he actually falls over his left foot and usually fails to get his right foot into the correct position at the centre of the circle, often piking at the waist in the process. This fault is caused by his failure to get fully on to his left foot and by picking up his right leg prematurely in the set-up.

To prevent this from happening, the athlete must ensure that his right leg remains planted at the rear of the circle until his weight has been fully transferred on to his rotating left foot. To achieve this he must attempt one or both of the following: either keep the right foot down for a longer period of time or turn the left shoulder, knee and foot, more quickly away from the throwing arm.

3. Piking at the waist: This fault commonly occurs, or is more obvious, during the drive across the circle and often accompanies over-rotation in the set-up phase. The hips break at the waist forcing the athlete to adopt an incorrect and inefficient throwing position at the front of the circle with a consequent loss of torque. The cause is often found in the early stages of the technique usually because the athlete adopts a leaning forward, seat out, type of stance which is continued into the rest of the technique. This causes the athlete to lean forward over the toe of his left foot when he moves into the set-up.

To combat this tendency to pike forward, the athlete should first be schooled into adopting the correct sitting position, with chest upright and hips forward in line, in his original stance. He must then ensure that he does not break at the waist in the wind-up phase; the result must be that the right hip leads the athlete into the set-up phase with the back remaining relatively straight and shoulders level.

4. Loss of torque: This usually occurs in the early stages of the technique, at the rear half of the circle. The athlete may perform an otherwise correct technique, but there is a failure in getting the lower half of the body to lead throughout. This commonly results in a loose, arm-only delivery with subsequent loss of distance and a tendency to remain 'too safe' within the front of the circle. The common cause is usually a failure by the athlete to understand and appreciate both the principle and the feel of locking the lower part of the body, especially the right leg, so that the upper part of the body can act in opposition in the wind-up and set-up stages. Often the athlete fails to leave the throwing arm behind by pivoting away with his left foot and knee just at the point where the throwing arm has reached its farthest position in the wind-up. A further cause of this fault is the athlete's attempt to achieve a maximum wind-up by throwing the discus arm backward as hard and fast as possible. The result is usually that the throwing arm rebounds and catches up with the rest of the body with a subsequent lack of torque.

The remedy of this fault will only be supplied if the athlete performs many drills involving the stages from stance to setting-up in an effort to obtain the correct timing in turning away when the throwing arm is kept at this farthest point.

Loss of torque may also occur in the centre part of the circle, despite a perfect execution as far as the set-up. This is usually caused by a slow action of the right leg in the drive into the centre of the circle. A common fault is to carry the right leg, rather than kick forward and clip the foot into a correct position in the centre. The obvious results of an ineffective right leg are that it causes the athlete to stop momentarily in the centre of the circle, allowing the throwing arm to catch up when the right foot fails to clip insufficiently beyond 180-degree turn.

The athlete must attempt to make this driving phase more effective by pushing off strongly with the left foot and maintaining an extremely active right leg, with the foot clipping-in beyond 180-degrees of rotation. He must also ensure that his left knee moves as close as possible to his right leg when it, in turn, transfers to the front of the circle in preparation for the delivery. Failure to do so will, again, slow the technique down with a resulting loss of torque upon delivery.

5. *Scooping the discus upon delivery:* This is a fault that can be found even in the most experienced athlete and refers to the tendency to deliver the discus from a point around the right hip, resulting in too high a delivery and subsequent lack of distance. This usually occurs when the athlete drops his left shoulder during the turn across the circle, resulting in a loss of balance which he usually attempts to correct by suddenly looking up and away from the direction of throw in the delivery. This causes the throwing arm to drop to a position close to the right hip, placing it in a mechanically unsound position to deliver the discus effectively. Care must be taken to ensure that the shoulders are kept in a square position throughout the technique.

6. Throwing off the rear leg on delivery: This usually occurs because the athlete inhibits his technique because of his fear of committing a foul by stepping out of the front of the circle. What usually happens is that he braces the right leg straight immediately it lands at the front of the circle, thus this leg does not assist the throw. This fault may also occur when the athlete attempts to look up towards the direction of the throw, before his left foot has contacted the ground at the front of the circle. Both faults result in an inefficient delivery due to the difficulties involved in applying his body weight and power behind the throw, which can only be corrected by adopting the correct positions and timing.

7. Faults occurring in the delivery: The most common of these is to turn the head away from the throwing arm upon delivery which results in a violent tug on the discus, away from the line of throw. This usually occurs because the athlete attempts to get a longer, but false, pull on the discus, and can only be corrected by 'looking' the discus away until it has left the hand.

8. Incorrect flight of the discus: Should the discus wobble after its release from the hand, the athlete must examine any faults which are occurring in the delivery, caused by an ineffective stabilizing action of the thumb and squeezing action of the fingers.

An incorrect angle of flight is usually due to a 'scooping' or 'bowling' action of the discus and is usually caused by faults earlier in the technique which have tilted the shoulders or altered the disposition of the throwing arm. If all is well in the rest of the technique, then the throwing arm should perform its action with the release occurring directly in front of the face, which should be looking in the direction of the throw.

Training to Throw the Discus

Basically a discus thrower must combine the physical attributes of height and weight with the physical qualities of strength, gymnastic agility, speed and suppleness. Although this event is the main province of the tall and heavy 'strong man', these qualities on their own are not nearly enough. It is a common sight to see the relatively smaller athlete compete with distinction among the big men, even to the point of beating them, purely because his gymnastic and balletic abilities enable him to secure a more efficient technique. Despite notions to the contrary, a gymnastic ability can be taught even to the most unlikely person if he has the all-important will to persevere with the necessary training.

A well-balanced and planned training programme, suitable to the individual's age, sex and sporting event, based on the general ideas set out in the earlier chapter on preparation training, must ensure that the athlete is fully prepared both mentally and physically for his athletic competition. In reading the schedules below, as with those in the other chapters, the athlete must take into account the fact that they are designed specifically for a male in his late twenties, 6 ft 3 in tall, weighing nearly 18 st (with little excess body fat), who is already a seasoned international and British champion discus thrower: Peter Tancred. Apart from those athletes who are in their early teens, this might only mean a suitable reduction of weights lifted, or a general reduction of the numbers in repetitions. Essentially, the amount and distribution of the time spent in training should vary only according to the specific needs of the athlete and the availability of suitable facilities.

All points not fully explained in this section may be clarified by looking back at the first chapter on preparation training.

SUITABLE EXERCISES FOR STRENGTH
(*Note:* for all weight-lifting the athlete is advised to make use of supporters ('spotters') for safety purposes; it is also advisable to wear a weight-training belt during some of the activities.)

Bench-press: possibly the most popular exercise with throwers because it is a 'safe' lift involving no problems of balance and therefore relatively little danger. The athlete lies down on a bench with a suitably weighted bar being placed at arm's length above his chest. Taking in a good breath, the athlete lowers the bar so that it gently touches the upper part of his chest, keeping his elbows directly under the bar in a strong position for the push. Immediately the bar touches his chest, the athlete pushes upward strongly with his arms, to return it to the starting position, at the same time exhaling (controlled breathing out). Care must be taken to ensure that neither the head nor hips are lifted from the bench at any time during the lift and that the feet remain firmly on the ground in a comfortable position either side of the bench. This exercise strengthens the shoulders, arms and upper chest and may be performed with a close or wide hand-grip (the latter being the most preferred).

The Clean: once again, a popular exercise for throwers because it combines the qualities of a brute, animal-like sense of attack (so loved by top throwers) with a good sense of co-ordination, necessary for the safe performance of this exercise. The athlete starts this exercise with a weighted bar on the ground. Placing both feet directly beneath the bar, at about shoulder width apart and with the toes facing slightly outward, the athlete then secures his hand-grip at roughly the same width as his feet (possibly a little wider). The athlete then half squats to a position where his knees go over the bar, while keeping his back flat and his head up, looking directly in front of him. Maintaining the flat back, head-up position and with straight arms, the athlete uses the explosive power in his legs to lift the bar to a point half-way up his chest. While the bar is moving fast at this point, a quick flex of the knees will lower the athlete quickly to a position where he can bend and swivel his arms to support the bar by the hands and upper chest. As this exercise is largely a matter of technique, it is important that the athlete should first acquire the timing by using relatively light weights. It should also be noted that if the back is not held straight, with head erect, then physical injury can occur. This exercise strengthens the legs, back, shoulders, upper chest and arms.

The Squat: in this exercise the athlete stands straight with a weighted bar placed across the back of his shoulders in a 'comfortable' position (padding can be used), the hands adopting a wide grip with the elbows pressed forward. The feet should be slightly wider than shoulder width apart and with the toes and knees slightly turned out. Taking a good breath and maintaining a straight back with the head up, the athlete flexes his knees into a squatting position. He may perform either a half squat where the seat lowers only a few inches, or a full squat where the seat lowers to a position slightly below his knees. It is important to note that throughout the exercise the heels remain firmly in contact with the ground and that the back is kept perfectly straight. It is also important to note that the athlete should not squat too low to a weak position that may cause injury. Straightening the legs while pushing the hips forward, with controlled breathing out, should return the athlete to his starting position. With careful 'spotting', this is an excellent strength exercise, mainly for the front of the upper leg (quadriceps).

Lateral Raise: this exercise may be performed on a normal bench or one that is inclined. Lying down on a bench, the athlete grasps a weighted dumb-bell in each hand and holds these straight out above his chest (if on an incline, then above the face). Maintaining a straight arm, the athlete lowers the weights to a position slightly below and to each side of the bench, while breathing in. As he breathes out he raises the weights, all the time maintaining a straight arm, back to their original position. Many athletes are seen performing this exercise with slightly bent arms, but we prefer to attempt to use straight arms because this more closely resembles the action in discus throwing. This exercise strengthens the arm, front upper shoulder and chest.

SUITABLE EXERCISES FOR SUPPLING

Cat-licks Performed in Box-splits: for this exercise the athlete must first achieve a standing position with his legs as far apart to the sides as possible, toes pointing outward (box-splits) and keeping the hips well forward. While maintaining this position, the athlete bends forward at the waist, placing his hands on the ground, until his nose is as close to the floor as possible. Walking forward on bent arms, with his nose close to the floor, the athlete should reach a position similar to that of a press-up. At this point, when the athlete's stretched hips are touching the floor, he straightens his arms slowly (with head looking up and back) to a position where his arms are straight, back arched, and hips remaining on or as close to the floor as possible. A complete reversal of this action will return him to his starting position. The legs must maintain the box-splits position throughout. An excellent suppling exercise for the front of the hips, lower back and inside leg, it simulates the hip position for delivery (except using both hips).

Arm Suppling: with the athlete sitting on the ground, both legs resting straight out in front of him, the arms are placed close together behind the back with the palm of each hand on the floor, fingers pointing away from the body. The athlete now attempts to 'walk' forward on his seat, keeping his chest out and head up, and leaving his hands in their original position, until the maximum shoulder range is achieved. Maintaining this position for about one minute, and with repetitions, he should increase the range of movement and subsequently the range of 'pull' that the throwing arm can exert on the discus.

SUITABLE EXERCISES FOR SPEED

Sprinting: the athletic discus thrower does not require the sprinter's ability to perform off blocks, so there is little need for using them (unless, of course, he is also an accomplished sprinter). Our preference is for the athlete to use a suitable running area, and surface, which allows at least 60 m of uninterrupted space. The athlete should place a marker at roughly 10 m distance from the starting point. The idea is then to jog fairly quickly to this marker and, upon reaching it, explode into a full-pace sprint which should be maintained throughout the remaining distance. The athlete should aim to reach maximum speed as soon after reaching the marker as possible, with the maximum degree of balance and control, remembering that the arms must punch as fast as the legs.

Jumping: any type of fast jumping exercise is suitable for fostering the type of leg speed required by the athletic thrower. These can range from fast and springy sets of tuck jumping (with their gymnastic-type quality) to the explosive standing 'broad-jump', and even to short-sprint, long or high jumping. As with all speed training, variety is the key to improved ability.

SUITABLE EXERCISES FOR STAMINA

Any exercise using the whole body which involves the athlete in a slightly-below-maximum rate of work over a period of time will serve to increase stamina. Increasing stamina involves the endurance of the athlete to perform work and therefore much 'stamina training' will be done outside the athletic season. This being so, the athlete may choose to promote his stamina by taking part in one, or even all, of the following activities.

Running: longer distances up to 1 or 2 miles. During the athletic season, however, the athletic thrower may be concerned to preserve his bodyweight, therefore the shorter distance (1 mile) at greater intervals (once, maybe twice, a week), would be sufficient. If the majority of stamina training is performed out of season, the hard competitive and pre-season training schedules should maintain suitable stamina levels, with the odd run to test and reinforce this.

Swimming: several lengths of a decent sized pool, performed at reasonable speed, are usually sufficient. Many people say that swimming loosens the muscles, making them soft and ineffective; we don't believe this myth and suspect that one would have to spend a great deal of time in the water for this to happen. Any muscle-relaxing effect it could have would probably be of great benefit to some of our tensely muscle-bound athletes, inasmuch as they would relax, preventing great wasting of energy and possibly improving their technique.

Games: squash, badminton, etc. will do much to enhance stamina as well as provide a good psychological break from 'necessary' training for the throwing events. The emphasis should be on enjoyment, which usually leads to an increase in general stamina.

Weight Circuits: involves a greater selection of exercises, performed with a greater amount of repetitions, which results in spending a greater amount of time. This promotes muscular stamina to a greater degree than the other activities above. Can be performed pre-season, and also during the season if required. Remember the emphasis is on endurance and not strength, therefore light and easily manageable weights are required. The amount and types of exercises are a matter for each individual athlete, but the complete circuit should balance out between shoulders, arms, stomach and legs, with no undue emphasis on any one part of the body.

PLANNED TRAINING
The way that any training is planned is a matter for the individual athlete, who should take into account the length of time out of season and the length of the competitive season. For convenience, we have split the full year's training into three-parts: Out of Season; Pre-season; Competitive Season.

Out of Season (September–December): After a period of recovery, in which the athlete may forget (temporarily) the past season's competitive efforts, his first thoughts are towards a period of conditioning. He may start this by taking part in games or activities such as squash, badminton or swimming, moving on quickly to weight training with the emphasis upon light loads and high numbers of repetitions, progressing towards occasional heavier weight sessions, with the emphasis upon heavier loads and less repetitions or pyramid training (explained in Chapter One). He will certainly be concerned with a heavy programme of suppling and, possibly, gymnastic-type activities. A typical example of a week's training may be as follows:

Day 1: Suppling, light weights, suppling.
Day 2: Suppling, gymnastic activity, stamina run, suppling, strength-in-extension.
Day 3: Suppling, heavy weights (small pyramids), suppling.
Day 4: Possibly some little technique or gymnastic training, suppling and rest.
Day 5: Suppling, light weights, suppling.
Day 6: Games or other activity (squash, etc.).
Day 7: Suppling, long run.

Pre-season (January–early April): During this period the athletic thrower will be initially concerned to raise the level of his strength and power and to begin serious work on technique training—especially that involving any radical changes in technique. Later on in this same period, the athlete will be concerned to maintain his high level of strength with the inclusion of more work on both speed and technique. He should still be equally concerned with suppling, especially as his increase in strength will build bigger, and potentially stiffer, muscles. A typical example of a training week at this point may be:

Day 1: Heavy weights, suppling.
Day 2: Suppling, technique training, strength-in-extension, suppling.
Day 3: Heavy weights, suppling.
Day 4: Suppling, speed training (sprints or bounding), strength-in-extension, suppling.
Day 5: Heavy weights, suppling.
Day 6: Short technique session, suppling and strength-in-extension.
Day 7: Technique training (some emphasis, later, on competition throwing), speed work and suppling.

(*Note:* there will be a gradual increase in the work-load, and thus differences in the type and distribution of training, from the beginning of this period until the start of the competitive season).

Competitive Season (May–August): By this time the athlete should be at the peak of his condition. He will be concerned only to maintain his levels of strength and suppleness, and only to refine his, by now, well-grooved technique. Training must now be phased with competitions in mind, with some emphasis between times upon speed and suppleness. The athlete should also be concerned to find out what is the best suitable rest period immediately prior to competitions (whether up to one week, or merely one day). Emphasis will be strictly upon refinements and reaching one's peak at the right time for the right competitions, followed by the analysis of performance and further (non-major) refinements in technique. As the training each week is a matter of individual taste and the number of athletic competitions, it is usual that training will be flexible and a matter between each athlete and his coach, therefore it is impossible to give a timetable for a typical week.

It should be remembered that planning is essential for training, not only because the athlete is likely as a result to be better prepared, and therefore more successful, but also for motivational purposes. It is essential to keep a diary in which each day's activities may be noted and examined in the light of future performance. Such planning pays dividends that mere sweat cannot.

III

Shot

History of the Event

There is no doubt that throwing activities, in a general sense, formed part of the activities undertaken by prehistoric man in his attempts to manipulate his environment and, more especially, in his attempts to secure food. Undoubtedly the most common missile available to early man was the ordinary stone and one may surmise that, before he used the stone to fashion more efficient implements, the crude stone itself was man's first weapon—and what better way to use it but by throwing it!

As primordial man became more aware of his fellow men there arose a need to establish a pecking order, so that the strongest could dominate without the need to kill or maim his fellows. In this primitive environment the ability to run, jump, lift heavy objects, fight and throw missiles was all important to survival and so it followed that the person who could do these best should stand at the top of the pecking order. Thus the earliest 'contests' took place and pride and prowess in throwing ability were established.

It is likely that throwing a weighted object preceded the evolution of the Greek style of discus throwing as an athletic event, but there appears to be little evidence as to the exact nature of this event. The earliest indications of an event which preceded shot putting are to be found in early Celtic history where they practised 'putting the stone'. This event was included in the Irish Tailteann Games, which began in 1829 BC. Putting the stone was still an activity practised by the English throughout medieval times up to, and beyond, the reign of Henry VIII, himself an accomplished athlete. Until the early nineteenth-century, weight throwing had little standardization and few restrictions on the competitors as to the style or manner of their throw. The weight was often thrown after an unlimited run-up, and a follow-through was allowed, provided that the weight was released before a line. Until the 1860s a two-handed throwing technique was employed (referred to at that time as the 'Oxford two-hands style') but after the 1860s the 'Cambridge one-hand style' became the standard method of throwing. This latter method of throwing featured in the first English Championships organized by the new Amateur Athletic Club in 1866, where attempts were also made to standardize the weight to 16 lb (7.25 kg), as it remains today.

There is little evidence to suggest exactly how the implement changed from the sacred stones, thrown by the Celts some 4,000 years ago, to the modern implement of today. It was usually the lot of the common man in the last century to be press-ganged into His Majesty's services, either Navy or Army. The bigger and stronger men were usually 'selected' for artillery work, where the large cannon used in that era of warfare had to be man-handled, along with the shot which was its ammunition. It takes only a little speculation to suggest that these men, in the spare time afforded by the slowness of warfare, were encouraged to compete in physical activities, one of which must have been throwing the shot, or cannon-ball. This, however, is only speculation on our part, but it seems reasonable to suggest such a case by virtue of the fact that we call the modern-day implement a 'shot'.

The advent of the first Modern Olympic Games in 1896 saw the domination of the shot putting event by the Americans, a domination which was to last until 1972. One American, 17-st (108 kg) Ralph Rose, dominated the event for more than a decade becoming twice Olympic Champion in 1904 and 1908, and establishing a world record put of 51 ft (15.54 m) in 1909, which was to remain for the next 19 years. It was in the 1908 Olympics, the first London-based Games, that the present-day 7 ft (2.13 m) circle was introduced. Once the 51-ft (15.54 m) barrier had been broken, by Emil Hirschfield with 51 ft 9⅝ in (15.79 m), a spate of record-breaking puts followed until Jack Torrance (USA) produced an astonishing put of 57 ft 1 in (17.4 m) at Oslo in 1934. Hailed as an invincible put which would finish all record breaking, this remained the record for 14 years until in April 1948 a comparatively light-weight American Negro, Charles Fonville, possessed of remarkable speed, strength and technique, produced an astonishing put of 58 ft and ⅜ in (17.69 m) to become a surprise record holder.

Before 1948 the standard technique of putting involved a strong trunk rotation, with the hips and shoulders twisting simultaneously towards the front at the point when the right leg began its drive. James Fuchs (USA) produced a variation of this technique in the 1949 Olympics. Fuchs delayed his trunk rotation by concentrating on a vigorous lateral whip upward of the body, combining this with a powerful lift of the right hip by the drive of the right leg, which occurs before the hips and shoulders are allowed to twist to the front. To ensure a good lateral 'pull' on the shot, Fuchs landed from his glide at a position with his back almost parallel to the ground and with his right elbow on the same horizontal plane as his right knee. A maximum upward stretch of the right shoulder, as the trunk became erect, increased the range of the upward sweep of the shot, and the delayed rotation to the front followed immediately. Once refined, this technique produced for Fuchs a record put of 58 ft 10¾ in (18.16 m) in 1950.

In winning the Olympic title in 1952 at Helsinki, another American, Parry O'Brien, added a further refinement to the Fuchs technique by starting his put facing square-on towards the back of the circle, his back thus facing the direction of the throw. This technique is universally copied by all putters of today, and remains the standard style of modern shot putting. With this technique O'Brien broke through the 60 ft (18.28 m) barrier in 1954, and went on to produce a phenomenal 63 ft 5 in (19.33 m) by 1960. The world record continued to be broken: in 1960 by Dallas Long with 64 ft 6½ in (19.67 m); by Bill Neider 65 ft 10 in (20.06 m) in the same year; and several other athletes added their names to the 60 ft plus role of honour.

In 1965 a nineteen-year-old American, Randy Matson, raised the world record to 70 ft 7¼ in (21.52 m), breaking both the 70 ft and 21 m barriers. The 70 ft mark remains the one by which all world-class throwers are judged today. A further technical innovation, however, appeared in the form of rotational putting, in which the thrower adopts a technique very similar to that of the discus thrower. Although many throwers experimented with this style of throwing, it was not until 1972 when Alexander Baryshnikov (USSR) used the technique to achieve a Russian record of 67 ft 4¾ in (20.54 m) that this form of throwing really began to be perfected and become popular. Unfortunately the technical perfection needed in order to achieve success with this technique often leads to minor errors which result in disaster, thus it is rarely seen in top-class competition.

One of the more recent refinements of technique, and one that remains controversial as regards its effectiveness, is the notion of 'pre-tension'. In this form of throwing there is an attempt to increase the duration of the delivery phase by extending and exaggerating the rotation of the upper body by turning the shoulders farther to the right, facing a position towards 1 or 2 o'clock in the starting position at the back of the circle. Although some athletes, notably Feuerbach (USA) and Winch (GB), achieve a great deal of success with this method, many athletes find that they cannot maintain such a high degree of torque when they enter the glide phase at the centre of the circle. Greater experimentation and the perfection necessary to add this refinement to the standard technique as practised by all throwers today may well result in a world record.

Breakdown of the Event

THE HOLD

The most common injuries in shot putting occur usually to the wrist or fingers, as a result of holding the shot wrongly. Although the hold will vary according to the wrist and finger strength of the performer, the ideal method that will provide the maximum propulsion with the fingers, but with the minimum of strain to the hand, is as follows.

To prevent undue strain to the hand, the shot is held high on the fingertips, with the fore, middle and third fingers reasonably close together. It is often preferred to curl the little finger round the shot to provide added stability, the thumb providing opposite support and further stability.

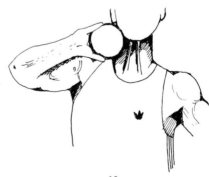

The conventional method of shot placement involves cradling (not actually holding or gripping) the implement beside the neck with the thumb touching the collar bone; the shot is thus rested between the neck and the jaw by the supporting fingers and the throwing arm is bent, with the elbow held high and almost parallel with the shoulder.

THE STANCE

The starting position may also vary according to the athlete's individual style. The most conventional method, however, is the one which we feel is the most natural. Starting from a position facing outward from the rear of the circle, opposite the direction of the throw, the athlete places his right foot with the toe facing inward, at a 12 o'clock position against the rim of the circle. The left foot is placed toe downward, approximately 12 in (0.3 m) behind, and slightly to the left of the right heel; thus the left sole is facing the direction of the throw. It should be stressed that the stance should be as comfortable and relaxed as possible in order to aid concentration. The right leg should be braced straight, with the weight firmly pinned on the heel,

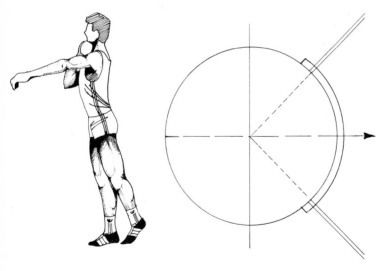

while the left leg is slightly flexed with the toe resting on the ground.

Before any movement is performed, the body assumes a relaxed upright position, the eyes focusing approximately 5 ft (1.5 m) away in a 1 o'clock direction, and with the shoulders parallel to the back of the circle. The right hand adopts the hold while the left arm assumes a relaxed position slightly below shoulder level and in front of the body, with the palm of the hand facing outward.

THE GLIDE

In preparation for the glide, the athlete drops his trunk over his braced right leg, taking the shot far outside the rear of the circle (providing maximum range). He bends his trunk forward and raises his left leg off the ground to assume a T-shaped body position. Without any hesitation the left flexed leg is dropped to bring both knees almost together, while the right leg flexes in preparation for the glide. This movement lowers the trunk and the athlete's centre of gravity, which is essential for the explosive movement that follows.

With the athlete's weight being firmly pinned on his right heel, the weight of his hips and unsupported left leg cause him to start to fall off balance towards the centre of the circle; the centre of gravity thus passes over a point behind his right heel. Just before the athlete would actually fall, the left leg executes a vigorous kick backward combining with a powerful rocking and pushing action off his right heel. The action of the left leg promotes speed across the circle, while the push-off of the right heel enables the right leg to be snatched up underneath the body prior to landing in the throwing position.

It is important to note that the athlete performs the kicking action of the left leg with the ball of the foot punching its way to the front of the circle, and not the back of the thigh or heel. The resulting action of the left foot will enable the toe to land at a position pointing towards the direction of the throw, giving the the desirable 'bandy' landing position. Initiating the kick with the thigh or heel often results in the toe facing towards the back of the circle, causing the athlete's hips to be prevented from turning into the delivery (i.e. blocking).

Throughout this phase, the athlete should focus his eyes towards the rear of the circle, so that his shoulders remain square to that direction. Because the hips are working in opposition to the shoulders, the athlete can help to maintain the correct shoulder position by keeping the coiled left arm at a position close to his right knee.

It is important for the athlete to keep his left side and arm as relaxed as possible during this movement in preparation for the explosive upward rotational action which will follow.

It should be remembered that in all throwing events speed is vital and shot putting is no exception to this rule. The speed is attained by the smooth and sequential acceleration initiated by the kick of the left leg. The fact that the hips are working against the shoulders produces the torqued position, allowing the shot to be kept outside and away from the right knee. This follows the principle of maximum force over maximum range resulting in maximum distance, a fundamental principle in all throwing events.

It is also important to remember that the head remains in the same horizontal alignment throughout this phase and that a conscious physical effort must be made to prevent the head looking away from its fixed focal point until the legs and hips have completed their action. Failure to do so will result in an up-and-down (bobbing) movement of the head and an ineffective position at the front of the circle. This bobbing of the head is usually accompanied by a failure of the feet to glide close to the ground, resulting in a hopping type of action. Such an action causes the shot to deviate, along with the application of power, from the intended flight-path. Such diversification may either produce an ineffective leg drive, because of the consequent high position, or for it to be poorly timed, because of the necessity to readjust the body position at the point when the front of the circle has been reached.

To help prevent this, the athlete may imagine that he is performing under a very low roof, which should prevent him from raising his upper body at any other time except at the front of the circle. In order to maintain torque, he may also imagine that a very strong elastic has been attached to his left wrist and is held by someone standing at a 3 o'clock position outside the circle.

The right foot, having completed its push from the back of the circle and at the point where the heel breaks contact with the ground, starts to invert (i.e. turns inward) in order to land at the centre of the circle with the toes pointing, ideally, towards a 9 o'clock position. This action causes the displacement between hips and shoulders, the lower half of the body being active while the upper half remains fixed. The key words are: shoulders and head 12 o'clock, right foot, knee and hips 9 o'clock.

THE THROWING (LANDING) POSITION

In completing the glide, the right foot should now be in a position at the centre of the circle and facing approximately towards a point between 9 and 10 o'clock. The left foot has landed behind the stopboard with the toes directly in line with the heel of the right foot (as in discus). This position of the feet permits the hips to remain open so that they can freely rotate towards the direction of throw. Failure to achieve the correct foot positioning may result in either blocking, or 'landing in the bucket', the former occurring when the alignment of the feet prevents the hips from turning, the latter where the left leg can provide no resistance to the drive of the right leg, preventing any effective 'chasing-out' and follow-through on delivery.

The athlete's eyes are still fixed on a position towards the rear of the circle, with both trunk and shoulders facing the same direction. He may help to slow himself down, or prevent any premature rotation of the upper body, by keeping his left arm downward and pointing towards the rear of the circle.

THE DRIVE TO THE POINT OF DELIVERY

With the left toe having now made contact with the stopboard at the front of the circle and with eyes still focusing on a point towards the rear of the circle, the athlete's body should be in the piked forward position adopted and maintained throughout the drive. In this position the athlete's body weight is pinned firmly over his right foot and his shoulders are square to the back of the circle.

From this point on, and until the wrist is about to execute its final flick against the shot, it is important that the athlete's feet do not lose contact with the ground. At this point in the technique the athlete has to perform a strong upward rotational movement of the trunk in order to arrive at an efficient point for the delivery. This movement starts with the simultaneous rotation of the right foot, knee and hip towards the direction of the throw. While this initial movement is being performed the athlete should keep his shoulders, and thus his throwing arm, facing towards the rear of the circle. Once the right hip has begun its vigorous rotational movement, the left arm makes possible a good open position of the left side by commencing to lead the left shoulder up and round, to complete the necessary rotation towards the direction of throw.

It should be stressed that this rotational unwinding is sequential in character (i.e. commencing with the right foot and knee and progressing upward to the trunk and shoulders), therefore the athlete should ensure that his focus is maintained towards the rear of the circle as long as possible and until all other body rotation is completed.

The nature of this rotational movement is such that the athlete's body weight remains firmly over his right heel; the drive of the right hip will therefore mean that his body assumes a 'bow' position. This can only be achieved by a vigorous upward and rotational drive, the hips moving underneath the shoulders and forward, while all forward momentum is limited.

The upward rotational movement of the shoulders should be accompanied by a movement of the elbow of the throwing arm outward and upward away from the chin. This movement ensures that the shot does not deviate from the line of throw, taken from the back of the circle and extended into the direction of throw. Having achieved the bow position with the body facing the direction of throw, a transfer of body weight brings the left leg into an active role. Until this point the left leg has been slightly flexed, but with the body weight starting to move on to it the athlete straightens it sharply into a braced position so that the forward momentum of the lower part of his body is halted, while causing greater acceleration to the upper part of his body, and the shot.

Many athletes disregard the action of the left arm throughout this phase of the throw. It must be emphasized that the left arm acts rather like a rudder to this part of the movement so it should move almost vertically upward and rotationally in order to prevent the position of the shot being brought inside the line of the right foot. It is desirable that the left arm should uncurl slightly for it to perform a wide arc led by the elbow, which helps to slow down the movement of the shoulders so that the vigorous hip rotation can be made more effective. In this movement the back of the left wrist passes in an arc over the forehead until both hips and shoulders are square to the direction of throw; at this point the arm and left shoulder are braced to prevent over-rotation. This bracing is helped by the athlete suddenly clenching his previously relaxed left hand. This locking of the left arm and shoulder should be performed simultaneously with the bracing of the left leg and hip so that the athlete's complete left side momentarily comes to a halt. The bracing action of the left side may also involve some backward movement of the left hip so the right hip can be brought into play much more effectively, thus giving greater driving force to the upper body, and also greater range to the delivery of the shot.

THE DELIVERY

Delivery is commenced after the bracing of the left leg has caused the acceleration of the upper body and shot. The position of the shot at this point has not changed, while the elbow assumes a high position in line and slightly below the shoulders. At the completion of the drive, the head and eyes have finally broken contact with their focal point at the back of the circle and are in the process of rotating towards the line of throw. It is important to remember that the head, rather in the fashion of a rudder, will dictate the flight-path of the shot, thus the athlete should attempt to maintain focal contact with the line of delivery until the shot has left his hand.

The final phase of delivery occurs with the strike of the putting arm. With the athlete now facing, and looking, in the direction of the throw, the right arm explodes upward and along the desired path of the shot. Throughout this movement the elbow is kept high so that it can transmit maximum force against the resistance of the braced left side of the body. As the arm extends forward the athlete's wrist is facing away from his right shoulder and this position is maintained until the arm, wrist and fingers are fully extended, applying maximum force against the shot. It should be noted that this complete movement is initiated by the right shoulder and, in sequence, ends with a flick of the wrist to ensure complete delivery by the fingers.

THE REVERSE
The nature of the delivery is such that the athlete attempts to 'chase' the shot out in order to ensure that maximum power has been fully exerted. This means the athlete starts to fall outside the stopboard at

the front of the circle. It is at this point that his right foot finally loses contact with the ground in order to execute the Reverse. It is important that this final scissor-like movement should not be operated until the shot has left the hand.

The chasing action of the athlete's right side causes his right leg to become fully extended until it reaches the point when it breaks contact with the ground, transferring his body weight up and over his left leg. As his right foot loses contact with the ground the athlete executes a scissor-like exchange of legs, so his right foot lands at the front of the circle with the outside of his toes against the stopboard. The left leg executes a wide and high arc which counterbalances the tendency of his body to fall outside the circle. Simultaneously the right knee is flexed to remove all remaining forward momentum, thus effectively preventing the athlete from falling outside the front of the circle.

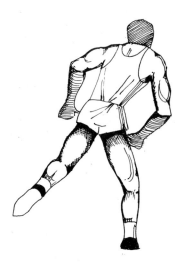

Throughout this chapter we have employed the technically correct term: putting the shot. It may be noticed that only when the drive to the point of delivery has been completed does the term 'putting' really apply. The majority of this technique requires that the shot is actually 'pulled' and then rotated across the circle. It is the fluid pull-rotation-put action of this technique that makes it extremely effective.

2

1

Faults and Corrective Procedures

1. Failure to adopt a correct stance: A common fault with the stance is a failure to adopt a good, relaxed flat back position before the glide across the circle. What usually happens is that the athlete rounds his back with the result that his chin almost makes contact with his chest, and the shot is lowered. This poor stance causes several mistakes to occur throughout the rest of the technique. First, the athlete often fails to focus his eyes towards a position to the rear and outside of the circle. Second, throughout the glide phase the shot travels in a lower horizontal line than is desirable. Lastly, on completion of the glide, the athlete usually adopts the same inefficient position immediately before the drive towards the delivery.

In order to correct this mistake the athlete should adopt the correct focusing position outside the rear of the circle and try to imagine that he is almost balancing a cup of hot tea on his flat back. Correctness in this position will ensure that the shot is neither brought 'around the corner', nor brought inside the line of the right foot in the drive before delivery.

2. Incorrect position of the throwing arm during the glide: Failure to keep the throwing elbow high and away from the athlete's right side throughout the glide usually results in two common faults. First, the shot is brought around the corner into the delivery position, and, second, the shot is 'slapped' on delivery, the wrist and hand snapping downward rather than sideways and away to the right. Often such a poor delivery results in pain and injury to the index finger of the throwing hand.

The athlete must ensure that the elbow is kept well away from the hip and outside the line of the right heel throughout the glide to the delivery. On the drive to the delivery the athlete should ensure that his elbow describes the widest arc possible.

3. Kicking the left foot to an incorrect position: There are two terms used to describe the faulty positioning of the left foot at the front of the circle: 'landing in the bucket' and 'blocking'. The first is caused by the athlete kicking the left leg to the extreme right of his supporting right leg. The latter is caused when he kicks too far to the left of his supporting right leg.

72

In order to correct this the athlete should ensure that his left knee closes to a position parallel to and close by his right knee, immediately prior to the glide. The adoption of this position ensures that the sole of his left foot is facing directly towards the line of throw. If the athlete then kicks his toe, and not merely the sole of his foot, towards the front of the circle this will further ensure that the left foot lands at the correct position. The athlete should also ensure that he is balanced and stable on his right foot immediately prior to his kick or the same mistakes may result.

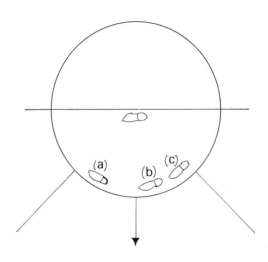

4. Premature opening of the hips at the centre of the circle: This fault usually occurs during the glide across the circle, but becomes more obvious as the athlete proceeds to drive into the delivery. Having initiated the kick with his left leg, and just at the point where his right heel is about to break contact with the ground, his hips turn prematurely towards the direction of the throw. Thus on landing, when he commences his drive, the shot is already inside the line of his right foot which means the upward rotation of his trunk is virtually impossible. His only alternative is to turn his trunk around a wide arc into the throwing position, so his left leg becomes inefficient in its attempt to brace immediately prior to delivery. This fault is usually caused by an unwinding of the left arm during the glide across the circle.

In order to correct this fault the athlete should ensure that his left arm is held slightly curled in front of his chest with his hand slightly above his right knee. He should further ensure that his hand remains above the right knee when it has clipped into the right position at the front of the circle, and also that his shoulders still remain square to the back of the circle. Failure to do so will result in a lack of pre-tension and spring-like quality immediately prior to the drive towards delivery.

5. *Premature reversing at the point of delivery:* This fault usually occurs when the athlete inhibits his technique through his fear of falling out of the front of the circle. What usually happens is that the athlete operates his switch before the right arm and hand have completed the delivery. This results in a loss of power due to the lack of resistance from the braced left leg when it should be in contact with the ground. This fault also prevents an adequate chasing out of the shot on final delivery.

In order to correct this fault the athlete should not attempt to inhibit his technique by not extending the left foot to the stopboard, or by leaving it passively flexed when it reaches a position at the front of the circle. He should concentrate on bracing his left leg effectively, with hips square to the direction of the throw, so the hinged upper body can be brought into play with great effect.

6. *Incorrect line of flight of the shot:* This fault usually occurs when the shot is either 'over-pulled', or 'under-pulled', at the front of the circle into the delivery. In over-pulling the shot, the line of flight is too far to the left, and in under-pulling the shot the line is too far to the right of the desired direction of put. Over-pulling is usually caused by the athlete failing to lock the left side of his body and breaking at the left hip at the point of delivery. Under-pulling of the shot usually occurs when the athlete fails to get his hips, and often his shoulders, square to the desired direction of putting at the front of the circle.

Over-pulling may be corrected by firmly bracing the left side throughout the delivery phase. Under-pulling may be corrected by ensuring that the hips execute a sharp 180-degree turn to face the direction of throw immediately before the right throwing arm is brought into action. If, despite the correct performance of the hips, the same faults still occur, the athlete should ensure that he is neither blocking nor landing in the bucket, as this may also result in similar faults on delivery.

7. Failure to invert the right foot after the glide: Failure by the athlete to clip his right foot into a position where his toes are facing to the left of the circle will result in one of the following: over- or under-pulling of the shot, slicing, or premature reversing. If the athlete fails to invert his right foot correctly the result will be an inability to achieve the accurate displacement between hips and shoulders, thus a reduction in the speed of the drive.

The only method of correcting this fault is by the constant repetition of drills to facilitate a smooth co-ordinated movement of the lower body and right foot in opposition to the shoulders. An effective practice of the glide phase may be achieved if the athlete secures an inner tube at a position roughly at chest height in front of him and then attempts to operate the technique while his shoulders and head are fixed on this point. This drill must be rapidly transferred to a practice using the shot if the correct skill is to be mastered.

8. Non-fluid movement at the centre of the circle: The most common fault at the centre of the circle is for the athlete, and the shot, to come to a premature halt immediately before the drive into the delivery. Stopping or slowing down at this point results in a loss of momentum and power to be applied to the shot.

The athlete must ensure that he lands on the ball of his inverted right foot in the centre of the circle and immediately continues without pause to begin his drive to the point of delivery. He must not be too high on the ball of the right foot or this will result in a loss of ankle extension important to the drive phase. The athlete should also ensure that his left leg kick from the rear of the circle is not too low, or this will reduce the time available to clip his right foot to a correct position underneath his body. He should not, however, over-rectify this mistake by attempting to kick his left leg too high.

Training to Put the Shot

Strength and explosive power, combined with the unchangeable attributes of height and length of levers (i.e. arms and legs), form the

75

major factors of importance to those athletes involved in putting the shot. Once again, however, we stress that a thrower is an athlete in the best sense of the word and should therefore be concerned to capitalize upon these major factors by paying some attention to those physical qualities not easily identified as being vital to the thrower.

In this section, and similarly in subsequent chapters, we shall be concerned to avoid repetition by detailing only those exercises which we feel are specific, or particularly valuable, to the event. Once again, you should refer to Chapter One for an outline of the basic principles and use these, in conjunction with your coach, to formulate a programme specific to your individual needs.

SUITABLE EXERCISES FOR STRENGTH

Inclined Bench-press: in this exercise the athlete lies down on an inclined bench, so that his back forms an angle approximately 80-degrees to the floor (i.e. nearly upright). The exercise performed is similar to that for normal bench-press (see Training to throw the discus) except that his body remains inclined throughout. The athlete should ensure that the weight travels vertically upward, and not outward, from the chest. This is a popular exercise with shot putters, because it almost resembles the type of action required for delivery, and strengthens those muscles of the arm, shoulder and upper chest necessary for this action.

Bent Arm 'Flyes': this exercise is the same as that given for Lateral Raises (see Training to throw the discus) except that the arms are bent as they are lowered to an angle slightly less than 90-degrees. This exercise may also be performed on an inclined bench and is ideal for strengthening the muscles of the chest and upper back.

Military Press: standing with the feet approximately shoulder width apart, the athlete either 'cleans' a weighted bar (see Training to throw the discus) up to his shoulders, or removes the bar from stands placed at chest height. From this position, and maintaining a straight back, the athlete pushes the bar vertically upward over his head until his arms are fully extended, and then lowers it back to the original position at shoulder height. For this exercise it is preferable for the athlete to wear a weight belt in order to protect the lower back. As well as strengthening the shoulders, this is an excellent exercise for strengthening the back. A more effective means of performing this exercise can be achieved by sitting on a bench; this prevents any cheating by preventing the athlete from using leg or body movement to assist the lift.

Dumb-bell Press: pressing with dumb-bells places more emphasis on strengthening the sides of the shoulders and may be performed standing, sitting, using both arms either simultaneously or alternately, and pressing with one arm only. This is an ideal exercise for strengthening and speeding up the action of the throwing arm, especially if the weight is moved at speed.

SUITABLE EXERCISES FOR SUPPLING
Cat-licks: this exercise is performed in exactly the same manner as for Cat-licks performed in box-splits (see Training to throw the discus) except that the legs are together throughout.

Trunk twisting: lie face downward on the floor with your arms held out sideways in the crucifix position. Take your right leg and swing it upward and over, twisting your hips in an attempt to touch your right hand. As far as possible, ensure that both shoulders remain firmly in contact with the ground and that the arms and other leg remain perfectly still. Repeat with the other leg. This is an ideal exercise for suppling the hips and lower back, so necessary for the delivery phase.

Quadriceps: possibly the most important part of the body to be suppled when one considers that stiffness at the front of the thigh often imposes a greater strain on the lower back and hips, usually resulting from heavy squatting with weights. An ideal exercise to stretch the muscles at the front of the thigh is for the athlete to kneel down, sit back on his heels and place his hands either on the floor behind him or rest them on his heels. From this position he pushes his hips forward as far as possible, so that his body forms a bow while maintaining contact on the floor with his hands or his heels. The head is held backward, to look at the ceiling, in order to emphasize the bow position.

SUITABLE EXERCISES FOR SPEED
Bounding and Sprinting: sprinting from either a standing, moving or

crouching start, over a maximum distance of 50 m (164 ft) is ideal for fostering leg speed. Because the action of shot putting involves a change of direction of the athlete's body, any sprinting activity which also involves change of direction is ideal for the purposes of training. Thus the athlete may jog in a straight line and, either at will or on command, sprint off in a different direction. Short and fast shuttle running is also ideal for this purpose because it involves the athlete in a process of changing direction at speed while starting from a crouched position.

Supplementary exercises, which involve the training of leg power/speed, can range from standing jumping (long, high, and triple) and variations of bounding and hopping.

Arm Speed: unlike discus and hammer and more like javelin, shot putting involves an explosive speed of the throwing arm, working from a bent (flexed) position towards a straight (delivery) position. To speed up this action of the arm the athlete must work on developing explosive strength rather than mere power when working with weights. By moving weights at speed, using exercises as specific to the putting action as possible, such explosive power can be developed. Many athletes concentrate on power alone, but this quality, although necessary, is not sufficient to project a missile the greatest distance; strength must therefore be developed in line with speed, and not at its expense.

SUITABLE EXERCISES FOR STAMINA

A properly planned training programme suitable to the athlete's level of ability will in itself, to a certain extent, foster the necessary stamina required for this event. For supplementary forms of stamina training, see the appropriate section in Chapter Two.

PLANNED TRAINING

Out of Season (September–December): In this period the athlete's main concern is to promote an all-round conditioning programme, which will build him up towards the heavier workloads which will follow. The major emphasis in this period will be on stamina, suppling and, to some extent, strength. The more advanced and experienced athlete may choose to work on certain aspects of skills training throughout this period but more especially towards the end. In this manner he may be better prepared for the more intensive throwing sessions which are vitally necessary for top performance.

The composition of his training week may change drastically, both in variety of content and in intensity, as he progresses towards his pre-season training. During the early part of this period he may be more involved in extra-curricular activities (e.g. squash, swimming, etc.); towards the end he will be concentrating a great deal more on skills training, throwing practice and strength training.

Pre-season (January–early April): It is during this period that the athlete will be more concerned to raise the level of his strength and begin serious work on technique training in his attempt to iron out any sources of major difficulty. Throwing sessions will become more dominant, and therefore more intense, and extra-curricular activities will have virtually disappeared (depending, of course, upon the nature and psychology of the individual performer). Towards the end of this period the athlete will be concerned to ensure that the power he has developed (through his intense strength-training) is equally matched by speed. Therefore, towards the end of this period he may concentrate a lot more on actual throwing for distance, and also upon suppling and speed training.

Competitive Season (May–August): The major concern of the top competitive thrower is to reach the peak of his ability and potential at those times when it is most vital (i.e. at major competitions). Therefore, the form and content of training during this period will depend upon the demands made by the athlete's competition schedule, and the advice of his coach.

In shot putting, the athlete's major concern is usually for the development and maintenance of maximum strength. It is often the case, especially after a poor performance in competition, that shot putters will have recourse to heavy weights many times during the competitive season. In our opinion, and in the main, this is often a mistake. First, maximum strength should never be confused with optimum strength, the latter often being less than the former in many of our top throwers. Second, reductions in strength (assuming the fulfilment of a well-planned and executed pre-season training session) are minimal provided the athlete follows a well-planned competitive programme. Major changes in technique should, at all costs, be avoided during this period.

(It should be noted that in this chapter, as in subsequent chapters, for further details involving preparation training the reader should refer to the relevant section in Chapter Two: Discus, and to Chapter One: Principles of preparation training).

IV

Hammer

History of the Event

In loose terms, the origins of hammer throwing may be traced back to the appearance of the sling during the Stone Age. As pointed out earlier in the history of the shot, man was preoccupied with hurling missiles in order to acquire food. Unfortunately the animals of that period were both hardy and ferocious and a missile projected solely with arm power often resulted in merely annoying the animal, which usually resulted in the hunter becoming the hunted. Man, being the ingenious creature that he is, decided that discretion was the better part of valour and that he must devise a method of projecting a missile from a greater distance, to enable him room for escape, and with greater force to cover the greater distance and retain enough impetus to ensure a kill. Whether by accident or by conscious design, there appeared on the scene an implement which, when whirled around the head, could project a missile with considerable force and over a considerable distance: the sling.

As with the shot, a hammer-type event was a feature of the Irish Tailteann Games around the period 2000 BC. The contest consisted of throwing either a complete chariot wheel or a single spoke of a wheel with the hub still attached. A closer brother to modern hammer throwing was the activity of throwing a sledge-hammer or blacksmith's hammer, which was contested throughout Britain during the seventeenth and eighteenth centuries and until the middle of the nineteenth century. Although more popular in Scotland, where it remains an event at the Highland gatherings of today, even Henry VIII, who featured in many athletic events, has been depicted 'throwing the sledge'.

The Scots have been credited with using a turning style of throwing prior to 1860, but this was discontinued because of the dangers of

81

premature release, and possible injury to spectators. The standard method of throwing used a 'pendulum' technique, the thrower standing side-on to his line of throw and swinging the hammer from side to side in front of him, releasing it from a standing position. The 'round the head' rotational style of throwing was said to have been introduced in the 1860s by one Donald Dinnie, but it is more likely that this style had been practised a lot earlier than this date. During the 1860s various experiments were made in hammer throwing: substituting a whippy wooden shaft, topped by a round iron ball, for the sledge-hammer; introducing a circular throwing area which changed in diameter from 7 ft (2.13 m) to 9 ft (2.74 m) and back again; and introducing a cross-piece or loop as a hand-grip.

In 1887, however, the Americans introduced standards for the event which remain very much the same as those that we have today. They set the maximum hammer length at 4 ft (1.22 m), the overall weight at 16 lb (35.27 kg), and allowed turns from a grass circle measuring 7 ft (2.13 m) in diameter. The hammer became an iron ball connected by means of a chain or wire to a triangular handle. The event was dominated at this time by a breed of Irish-Americans who, because of their size, were nicknamed the 'Irish Whales'. For 10 years from 1872 one James Mitchell dominated the event, achieving a world record of 145 ft 3¾ in (44.25 m) in 1892. Another Irish emigrant John Flanagan succeeded Mitchell as world record holder with 150 ft 8 in (46 m) in 1897; he subsequently went on to break the 160-ft (48.75 m), 170-ft (52 m), and 180-ft (55 m) barriers, and achieved a personal best of 184 ft 4 in (56.25 m) while still in his early thirties! Flanagan also achieved the almost incredible triple by winning the 1900, 1904 and 1908 Olympic Games—a feat only equalled by Al Oerter in the discus—and, apart from a brief period, he retained the world record for sixteen years! Another notable Irish Whale was Pat Ryan who, in 1913, achieved a world record of 189 ft 6 in (57.75 m), a record which stood for 25 years!

Until the 1930s the method of delivering the hammer involved the use of a 'jump' turn in which the thrower lost contact with the ground immediately before delivery. With the emergence of Germany as a hammer-throwing power in the mid 1930s, however, the jump turns were rejected in favour of the now modern technique of heel and ball-of-the-foot turning in which the thrower maintains contact with the ground throughout the throw. In 1938 Karl Hein broke Ryan's old record with a throw of 191 ft 1 in (58.24 m), a record which stood for 6 days, after which his fellow competitor, another German, Erwin Blask threw 193 ft 7 in (59 m) which remained the record for 10 years.

It was during the post-war years that the hammer-throwing explosion took place, both in terms of technical performance and in terms of popularity. Hungary appeared on the scene, in the shape of Imre Nemeth, who won the 1948 Olympic Games and went on to break his own world record 3 times until in 1950 it stood at 196 ft 5 in (59.86 m). Two years later Jozsef Csermak, at only 20 years of age, broke the 60-metre barrier with a throw of 197 ft 11 in (60.34 m) to win the Olympic Games in Helsinki in 1952. Two months later a Norwegian, Sverre Strandi achieved the first throw beyond 200 ft (61 m) with 200 ft 11 in (61.28 m); a year later he improved this to 204 ft 7 in (62.4 m). It was around this period that concrete circles began to replace the old grass or cinders, which also allowed for the development of the ultra-light and faster unspiked shoes of today. Another reason for the boom in athletics, and hammer throwing in particular, was the emergence of a new power: Russia.

The Russian system of early selection, athletic programming and coaching of athletes into appropriate events introduced a more scientific approach to the sport, which was to reap dividends. In 1954 a 25-year-old Russian, Mikhail Krivonosov, during the European Championships introduced a new technical concept of hammer throwing which was to herald the more advanced techniques of today. Until then, competitors tended to let the hammer lead the thrower into each turn, resulting in a passive or 'free-wheeling' action. Krivonosov demonstrated the advantage of leaning away from the hammer and leading it with the body throughout the turns so that at no time was there a slack or passive phase. By progressively overtaking the hammer at an earlier point in each turn, when the right foot was coming down, Krivonosov accelerated the hammer in a constant progression from the start of his first turn right up to delivery. With this method he first achieved a new world record of 207 ft 9 in (63.36 m), and with competition from another Russian, Nyenashev, 210 ft 1 in (64.07 m), went on to achieve a world record of 216 ft (65.85 m) in 1956.

At this point the two great powers, America and Russia, came together to do battle. America's Cliff Blair opened his account with 216 ft 4 in (65.95 m), which was answered by Krivonosov four days later with 217 ft 9 in (66.38 m). Harold Connolly then joined the battle with Krivonosov and, despite a withered left arm, finally surpassed the Russian's latest 220 ft 10 in (67.32 m) throw with a record distance of 224 ft 10 in (68.54 m). Connolly had made an intense study of the German method of being in advance of the hammer head, and improved this technique by emphasizing the importance of correct swings to maintain a more effective dragging lead, utilizing great leg strength to perfection in his delivery. He achieved this by turning on the outside of his left foot and sinking progressively deeper into a squatting position with each turn, this resulted in a tremendously powerful leg lift which, combined with a long unwinding of the hips and shoulders upon delivery, provided tremendous pull on the hammer head.

Since this period many great names have perfected the technique and, in combining the agility and co-ordination of the gymnast with the speed of the sprinter, have progressively raised the distance achieved in world hammer throwing. Gyula Zsivotzky (Hungary) achieved a phenomenal distance of 241 ft 11 in (73.74 m) in 1965 and improved this to establish the world record at 242 ft (73.76 m) in 1968. No doubt the substitution of the smaller diameter tungsten ball for the old-fashioned cast-iron hammer accounts, in part at least, for the dramatic improvement in world class performance today. Taking into account the limited size of an athletic stadium, further improvement may possibly make necessary either shorter wires or an even heavier implement.

SAFETY ASPECTS

The hammer can be a lethal missile and the rules are good common sense on this point. It is emphasized and re-emphasized that the only place on the field from which an implement can be thrown is the throwing circle itself, and all concerned can therefore keep a wary eye on this spot, at least safe in the knowledge that hammers will not be arriving from all directions. During a competition the number of officials in the landing area should be as few as possible and each should know where the others are. Competitors should not wander into the area because they become unknown hazards to any official who may suddenly need to move out of the way of an implement. Safety throwing cages are important, but athletes and officials should make allowance for the 'give' of the netting and should not stand too close to the cage. Similarly, roped-off landing areas help to prevent accidents, but it should be appreciated that a wildly-thrown hammer cannot recognize sector lines or ropes and the best advice is to watch the hammer at all times.

Breakdown of the Event

THE GRIP

It may be seen from the photographs that a glove is worn on the left hand; this is done in order to prevent any painful friction burns to the fingers. This glove is an essential item of equipment and may be regarded as being vitally necessary for anyone contemplating performance in the hammer event.

With the hammer wire fully extended in front of him, the athlete inserts his gloved left hand inside the hammer handle to a position where the handle grip lies across the middle pads of the fingers. The right hand is then inserted on top and overlapping the left hand, in a supporting role. Having achieved this grip, the experienced athlete will allow the handle to slide down the fingers of his left hand so that it lies across the top pads so that the maximum effective range will be achieved throughout the technique.

THE STANCE

The athlete starts with his back facing the direction of throw as for shot and discus. The feet are placed with the toes flush against the rim at a distance slightly wider than shoulder width apart, in order to provide greater stability.

The athlete then drops his seat slightly to assume a sitting position. It is helpful for him to imagine that he is about to sit on an imaginary high chair. It is important that the hips are kept forward, with the knees flexed, so that his weight is firmly pinned over the heels of both feet (i.e. flat footed).

PREPARATION FOR PRELIMINARY SWINGS

It should be noted that for the right-handed thrower the direction of the swings and turns will be anti-clockwise. There are two fundamental methods for setting the swings into motion, the performance of which are as changeable among performers as ladies' clothing fashions.

The first is best described as the 'static-start'. With this technique the athlete takes the hammer, in his left hand only, from a position in front of his body and swings it to his right so that the hammer head comes to rest just to the right of his right heel. If the hammer is placed behind the right heel then on commencement of the swing the hammer head may make contact with the back of the right leg. It must also be stressed that the hammer wire is under tension immediately the technique is commenced so that the athlete should be in firm contact with the hammer head at all times. With the hammer resting on the ground to the right of the athlete, he now secures his grip with his right hand, and from this static position he commences his preliminary swings.

The second alternative is called the 'pendulum swing' start. In this technique the athlete secures his grip with his left hand while the hammer head is resting on the ground on his left-hand side. Lifting

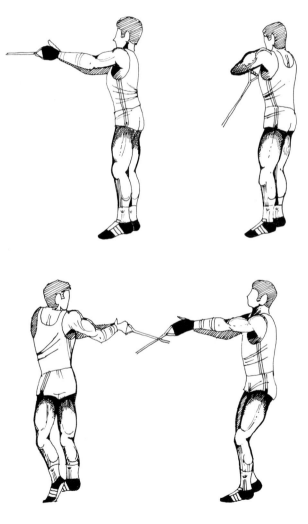

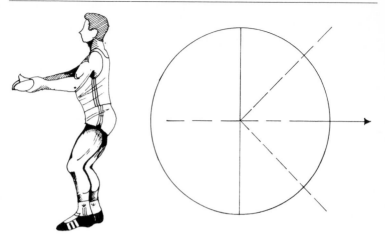

the hammer upward and forward to the front, the athlete then secures a grip with his right hand and without pause the hammer is swung downward and backward to the right of his body. The athlete then begins to perform his preliminary swings, using the resulting forward momentum from this pendulum-type action.

Our preference is for the pendulum type start as it assists continuity in beginning the swings, as well as minimizing excess muscular tension in the athlete's upper body. A further advantage of this technique is that it enables the lower part of the body to initiate the lifting movement of setting the hammer into motion.

THE SWINGS

With the hammer head now set in motion and moving upward and outward from a position to the right of the athlete, his arms are now straight and, at the point when the hammer head passes in front of him, he transfers his weight on to his left foot. The transfer of weight allows the athlete to rise on to his right toe allowing the right hip to assist in the lifting movement, setting the hammer in motion.

As the hammer rises in front of the athlete's face and immediately before it moves over his left shoulder, the athlete bends his arms at the elbow allowing his hands to travel across the right side of his forehead (never behind the head). Simultaneously, the athlete rocks back on to his right heel preparing to transfer his body weight. This movement results from the fact that his own left shoulder becomes the centre of rotation.

At the point when his hands are passing in front of his forehead and the hammer head is passing behind his back, the athlete begins to rise on to his left toe allowing his hips to lift and turn towards the right. The trunk twists to the right to face away from the direction of the hammer. Simultaneously, the left knee drops inward towards the right knee ensuring the smooth transition of body weight on to the right leg, further permitting 'hip contact' with the hammer throughout the swings.

As the hammer drops towards a low point at the right rear of the athlete the left heel regains contact with the ground while the right foot rises on to the toe. This complex rocking action of the feet allows the hips and upper body of the athlete to move, 'hula-hoop' fashion, to provide greater radius of movement to the hammer head as well as greater stability to the balance and counter-balance function of the lower body. It should be noted that the actual low point of the hammer, approximately 2 in (5 cm) from the ground, occurs at the front right just as the athlete's hips come back to face the rear of the circle.

The second swing is executed in the same way as the first, only now the rhythm changes slightly as the performance is speeded up to give increased, progressional acceleration causing the high point of the swing to become steeper. The arms and shoulders must remain relaxed as any sudden muscular contraction or change in balance would adversely influence the desired orbital path of the hammer head. The athlete should be aware that the purpose of the swings is to overcome the inertia of the hammer, to convert the movement of the hammer head on to a circular path, and to give it momentum prior to the turns.

Once the hammer has been lifted into motion it should never be 'pulled' but merely 'hung' as a natural extension of the athlete's arms. The term pull means an inward contraction (i.e. centripedal) by the arms and shoulders, rather than allowing the hammer to extend into its natural centrifugal action. It should also be noted that the arms and shoulders remain muscularly passive, so the majority of physical effort should be provided by the muscles of the lower body.

THE TRANSITION
This phase of the throw is best described as the link between the swings and the first turn, the part of the throw where the hammer head

travels from a position at the right rear of the athlete, around and up to
the next high point. As the hammer and arms are travelling downward
from a point over the athlete's right shoulder the body weight is
quickly transferred on to the left foot. This slightly early transfer of
weight results in a flattening in the plane of the swing. As the hammer
passes to the front of the athlete, he adopts a high 'sitting' position in

order to counter-balance the outward pull of the hammer. At this point the left hip starts to turn away from the hammer while the left foot lifts on to its heel to rotate in the same direction. The object of this delicate movement is for the athlete to get ahead of the hammer in preparation for the actual turns. At the transition stage most of the athlete's weight should be on his left heel, which is attempting to turn so that the toe will face the direction of throw; the right foot has lifted up on to the toes enabling the right hip to turn towards the left of the circle. He should commence to turn on the left heel at the moment when the hammer reaches its low point to the right of the right leg.

The timing of the transition stage should be such that the body does not enter prematurely into the turn (i.e. before the hammer head reaches its low point), nor should it be executed so late that the hammer starts to overtake the body.

The Turns

(a) *Foot movement and positioning:* Although some athletes may employ four turns, for reasons of simplicity, we believe it better to describe three turns because the problems of creating increased acceleration of the hammer head within the confines of a 7-ft (2.13 m) circle create even greater complexities in an already highly technical and complex event.

91

The turns are executed primarily with the heel of the left foot and the ball of the right foot, hence the phrase 'heel-and-toe turn'. His body weight is pinned firmly on his left heel, which is turning so that the toes are attempting to face the direction of the throw (180-degrees), the right foot pivots so that it points towards the left heel. This movement has now caused the flexed right knee to turn and face the back of the left leg prior to lifting the right foot off the ground; this ensures that the knees will remain relatively close together in the movement to follow. The right foot now breaks contact with the ground and the left foot rocks forward on to the toe and continues to pivot in this manner until the athlete has executed a 360-degree turn, whereupon the right foot regains contact with the ground, square to the back of the circle. The right leg should not be picked up too high off the ground, but should be raised sufficiently high to maintain balance. Throughout the turn it is important to remember to keep the right knee as close to the left as possible in order to prevent any slowing down caused by a sweeping action of the right foot.

The contribution of the right leg in the turns is fundamentally threefold. First, throughout all the turns the body weight should be centred over the left foot, therefore the right leg should be thought of as an instrument to assist stability; second, it helps in maintaining right-hip contact with the hammer; third, it checks any over-rotation. Thus the action of the right foot until the point of delivery is merely to 'caress' the ground rather than to bear the athlete's weight.

It may appear from the photographs that the athlete performs the turns on the outside edge of the ball of the left foot. Although this is true of the proficient, confident thrower, it should never be practised by any athlete during the initial learning stages. This action of turning is naturally acquired through good controlled balance. It may also be noticed that from the initial stance, where the feet are approximately shoulder width apart, throughout the turns and until the delivery the feet come progressively together to a point where they are approximately 12 in (0.3 m) apart. This shortening of the base provides increased acceleration and helps facilitate a good two-legged drive on delivery.

(b) *Body movement and positioning:* Ideally the thrower is endeavouring to get his hips and feet slightly ahead of his shoulders on the first turn, slightly more on the second, then really away on the final turn in order to gain a maximum torqued position. It is this rhythm which the athlete is working for, but not to the neglect of balance and poor positioning.

Throughout each of the turns the hips remain forward and should lead into the whole technique whereby the legs should be flexed so that the athlete's centre of gravity remains low, thus giving greater manoeuvrability within the circle. Throughout the technique the whole of the right side acts as an imaginary vertical post so that any lateral bend to the right or flexing of the hips is prevented. Such hip movement, although giving the sensation of an increased radius of the swing, would in fact reduce the range of the hammer head, thus causing the radius to be reduced also.

As the hips lead the technique, the relaxed shoulders and arms remain behind, the left arm being wrapped closely across the chest. Most athletes and coaches recommend that the arms should be kept as straight as possible. Without appearing to be controversial, we feel that a slight bend of the right arm will enable the athlete not only to 'get away' from the hammer more effectively by ensuring a better wrap across the chest, thus providing greater potential torque, but also (through shortening the radius of rotation) will increase the rotational acceleration of the turns. It is also our belief that the

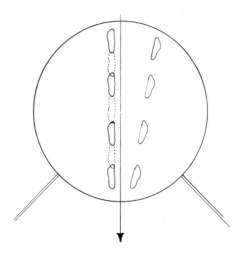

balanced management of this potential increase in speed, coupled with the skilful transition from bent to straight arms immediately before the right foot makes contact with the ground before delivery, will provide greater impetus to the hammer head and thus greater potential distance.

The essence of the turns in hammer throwing, as opposed to the movements performed in other throwing events, is one of balance supplied by the athlete's attempt to counter-balance the efforts of the hammer to escape his grip.

THE DELIVERY

The athlete's turns have resulted in a build-up of speed and displacement that has now to be converted during the delivery phase. As with the other turns, and at the point where the athlete's right foot is coming down on to the ground, the hammer is being accelerated both by gravity as well as by the rotational movement.

At this point, immediately before the hammer descends to its low point, the left leg is bent to provide for a deeper downward pull on the hammer wire. As the hammer descends from the rear right hand side of the athlete, the right foot is brought into firm contact with the ground. Thus the athlete is ready, with both legs flexed into a sitting position, to provide a maximum lifting force once the hammer has achieved a low point to the right front of his body. Until this point his weight has been firmly pinned on his left leg, but just when the hammer is passing its lowest point his weight is momentarily transferred on to his right foot in order to provide a two-legged drive.

From this squatting position the athlete continues to turn into the throw with his shoulders while the left leg locks straight to provide the fulcrum for the throw. The athlete, in delivering the hammer with straight arms, looks up and over his left shoulder towards the line of flight, relinquishing his grip at the point when he has risen on to the toes of both feet.

THE RECOVERY

Unlike discus and shot, the recovery phase in hammer throwing is a matter of feel and natural ability rather than a standardized technique. Thus recoveries vary from attempts to continue rotation or spin on the left foot to attempts to drop the centre of gravity by driving the hips backwards and 'sit' out of the circle.

2

1

10

9

11

Faults and Corrective Procedures

Hammer, because of its highly technical and complex nature, lends itself quite readily to a greater number of potential faults. Because of its emphasis on balance and rhythm, any slight movement which upsets these becomes a major fault in itself. The number of actions which can cause upsets are too numerous to detail. Therefore, it is even more desirable to have the keen eyes of a coach available to you in training, to correct what may at first appear to be trivial mistakes.

1. *Failure to initiate sufficient heel turn in the transition phase:* This fault occurs when the left foot fails to execute a 180-degree turn so that the toes face the direction of the throw. This is usually caused by the premature picking up of the right leg from the back of the circle. Such a fault causes the athlete to deviate from his line of progress across the circle towards the direction of throw (i.e. diagonally to the left of the circle).

The athlete must attempt to point the toes of his left foot directly towards the front of the circle before allowing his right foot to break contact with the ground throughout the transition and the turns.

2. *Over- and under-rotation in the turns:* Over-rotation occurs when the athlete executes more than a 360-degree movement in the turn, which results in the right foot being placed at a position in advance of the left so the athlete is no longer square to the back of the circle. This is caused by a failure on the part of the athlete to achieve the correct foot placement, due either to excessive weight bearing on the left foot, or his anxiety to commence subsequent turns.

Under-rotation occurs in the same movement, but in this case the athlete has failed to execute a complete 360-degree turn. His right foot has slowed to land in a position slightly to the rear of the left leg. This is usually caused if the athlete attempts to lean away from the hammer and lead the movement with his left shoulder. The resulting imbalance towards the centre of the circle causes the premature pick up and placement of the right foot in order to regain his equilibrium.

Under- and over-rotation, or any misplacement of the right foot, not only causes the athlete to travel diagonally across the circle, but will also cause the hammer head to describe a misplaced elliptical path which has disastrous results, often on delivery.

An ideal practice to correct this movement is for the athlete to place a broom handle or bar across his shoulders (keeping them straight) and to stand straddling a line on the floor. He may now execute one or multiple turns and check the position of his feet in relationship to the line.

This drill may also be used to check the performance of the left foot. To do this the athlete places this foot on the line and checks to see that it still contacts the line after the execution of his turns. He must attempt to point and pivot his left foot along the line in order to achieve the desired progress towards the front of the circle.

3. *Failure to achieve a low position:* This fault usually occurs throughout the turns, when the athlete fails to sit into the correct 'high chair' position. Often what happens is that the athlete leans forward at the waist, causing his seat to stick out behind him. This is often accompanied by the fact that he looks down towards the ground, providing himself with a false sense of positioning.

This fault is usually the result of a lack of confidence in his own balancing ability. Often it is a habit acquired during the learning stages when the athlete looks down to check not only his foot positions, but also his whereabouts.

To correct this fault the athlete must adopt the right body posture immediately he commences the transition, ensuring that his chin is not in contact with his chest. He may also try to imagine that the ground does not exist, therefore his only reference points exist at eye level.

4. *Failure to achieve the correct low point:* In order to execute a correct delivery the athlete must ensure that the hammer head achieves a low point (not more than 2 in (5 cm) from the ground), at a position just to the right of the right knee as the athlete is facing the rear of the circle. Failure to achieve this low point results in the trajectory of the hammer being flattened out throughout the turns and thus a failure to achieve a suitable high point so vital for an efficient delivery.

This is usually caused by the athlete's failure to allow his hips to face square to the back of the circle after the execution of each of the turns. The athlete must ensure that, when his right foot makes contact with the ground, he allows a certain amount of unwinding before using his hips to wind up again into the next turn. He must not attempt to enter subsequent turns prematurely as this will result in a premature pull on the hammer head and raise the low point to a height where it becomes inefficient.

5. *'Hooking' on delivery:* The term 'hooking' refers to the type of movement caused by a breaking at the right hip upon delivery. This is usually the result of incorrect balance causing excessive weight bearing on the right foot throughout the turns, and a failure by the athlete to maintain the majority of his weight on the lifting left leg at the point of delivery.

Training to Throw the Hammer

Contrary to popular opinion, hammer throwers do not need to be giant strong men, with excessively long arms. Co-ordination and balletic ability pick out the top hammer thrower from many of his contemporaries, and from the majority of athletes involved in other throwing events. It is usually the case that the taller and stronger man lacks the co-ordination and balletic quality so vital for executing the hammer throwing technique. This is possibly why the majority of hammer throwers are under 6 ft 3 in (1.9 m) in height. Indeed, many world class performers are under 6 ft. Strength alone can never compensate for a lack of balletic ability, as may be the case in other throwing events. Speed, style, and co-ordination, combined with a gymnastic-type application of power are the major qualities vital to this event.

SUITABLE EXERCISES FOR STRENGTH
The Squat: this may possibly be regarded as the most vital strength training exercise for hammer throwing, when one considers that the complete technique (apart from delivery) is performed in a semi-squatting position. For details of performance refer to Chapter Two.

Bent-over Rowing: the athlete bends at the waist and takes a grip upon a barbell directly below his shoulders on the floor. From this position he raises the barbell from the floor and lets it hang with his arms extended and his body bent at right angles (parallel with the floor). Bending his arms, he pulls the bar upward to contact his chest, maintaining a flat back throughout, and then lowers it to return to the straight arm position. Although the arms remain straight throughout the hammer throwing technique, there is a great deal of need for strength in the middle and upper back, which this exercise superbly provides.

Deadlifts: the athlete adopts a straight-legged position, similar to that for bent-over rowing. The object of this exercise is to lift the weight by straightening into an upright position while maintaining straight arms. Standing with his feet a little wider than the width of his shoulders, head up and back flat, the athlete bends down to take a grip on the bar and, taking a deep breath, pulls the bar upward until he is standing vertical with his arms straight and the bar at hip height.

Although we have included this exercise because it is ideal for strengthening the back, we feel that lifting excessive loads in this manner can cause serious, and often permanent, damage to an athlete's back, so care should be taken to ensure the correct poundage for the athlete's strength and stage of development.

Hyper Extensions: the athlete lies face downward on a high bench with his upper body extended over the edge and his feet locked firmly together and anchored, either by having someone hold them or by using some other method. From this position, the athlete clasps his hands behind his neck and raises his trunk up as far as he can (the complete reverse of a sit-up). This exercise is ideal for strengthening the back and is preferable to the deadlift. The stronger athlete may clasp a weight against the back of his head. This exercise may be varied by turning the trunk alternately to left and right as the upper body is being raised.

SUITABLE EXERCISES FOR SUPPLING

Hip Circling on Rings: in this exercise the athlete hangs from a pair of gymnastic-type rings (or even one ring), fully stretched and with his feet not touching the floor. From this position, and with his legs clamped firmly together throughout, he should attempt to perform with his feet a circling action that will get progressively larger, while keeping his arms long and relaxed and as still as possible throughout. This circling action is performed in a clockwise, and then in an anticlockwise, direction. The complete exercise closely mirrors the necessary suppleness of the hips and lower back that is required in the actual hammer throwing technique.

'*Bridging*': for this exercise the athlete lies on his back, bending his legs so that his heels touch his seat, and placing his hands, palms downward, flat on the floor at a position either side, and close to, his head, with the fingers pointing towards his shoulders. From this position, the athlete straightens his legs and arms and drops his head backward to look at the floor. Ideally, he should achieve a position with his back completely arched and his legs and arms perfectly straight. This exercise, if performed correctly, not only promotes suppleness in the back but, more importantly, in the shoulders (stiff shoulders frequently result in incorrect performance of this exercise). As an alternative, this exercise can also be performed while holding on to a low wall-bar.

SPEED

Hammer throwing is probably the most complex out of all the throwing events in terms of mechanical and physical movements. The complexity of the event often leads athletes into the mistaken idea of increasing muscular effort during performance in order to increase speed. Controlled relaxation is possibly the greatest key to successful increases of speed without adversely affecting technique. Therefore the athlete should carefully consider the manner by which he is seeking increased speed, taking into account the fact that maximum speed is no substitute for a correctly timed, co-ordinated and relaxed performance.

SUITABLE EXERCISES FOR STAMINA

In order to sustain a high standard of technical excellence throughout training for this event, it is vitally important for the athlete to be fit in terms of endurance. The repeated performance of the hammer throwing technique puts considerably more demands upon the athlete's endurance than do other throwing events. Lack of endurance fitness not only leads to a faster breakdown in terms of skills, but also places the athlete in danger, due to the nature of this event. A 16 lb (7.25 kg) hammer, travelling at speed, has little respect for a tired performer!

To a certain extent, the gradual build-up from gentle training sessions towards more intense training sessions will foster the necessary endurance. Supplementary training methods may be found in Chapter Two.

PLANNED TRAINING

The general construction of a training programme for hammer throwing will differ little from that given already in Chapters Two and Three. The only major differences will occur in the degree of emphasis placed on particular aspects of training. In our opinion, a hammer thrower should concentrate more heavily on gymnastic-type activities, which will foster the necessary co-ordinative ability so vital for this event.

V

Javelin

History of the Event

From the wooden shaft used to hunt fish in Sumatra to the warrior spear (assagai) used in ceremony by the Zulu tribes in Africa, the evidence for the origins of the javelin lives on even today. The javelin, like many athletic events, evolved from a need to hunt, kill and defend; as such it was developed initially as a lethal weapon. Once again, the means of establishing seniority in early civilization depended greatly upon man's skill to hunt and kill. In those early days, the contests that took place were many and various—throwing for accuracy, or for distance, from standing or from horseback. The spear, or javelin, figured greatly as a weapon for hunting or for war, as evidenced by early Egyptian and Greek artefacts. Its usefulness as a weapon, however, began to wane as early man realized that, having dispatched the spear, the thrower was powerless to keep his adversary at a distance or to kill him. This led to the development of the lance, which could be retained in continuous battle, and to the African-type blow-dart, which could be carried and dispensed in greater numbers.

The javelin remained, however, a means of establishing skill, strength and prowess in warrior-like activities, since its inclusion in the ancient Olympic Games in Greece. Artistic evidence also suggests that the manner and nature of those early competitions was extremely similar to that of today. The only notable difference was the use of a leather thong as an artificial aid. This thong was wound round the javelin and, with the free end held by the competitor, the result upon release was that the javelin was caused to spin, thus adding stability to its flight. Further evidence suggests that this event was popular in England during the Middle Ages, but courtly advice to practise with the then weapons of war, the long-bow and lance, led to its demise as a sporting pastime until more modern times.

In the intercalated Olympic Games of 1906 (held to celebrate the tenth anniversary of the revival of the Olympiads), javelin throwing was revived. It was a Scandinavian, Erik Lemming (Sweden), who established the winning throw of 175 ft 6 in (53.49 m), and went on to take the world record up to 200 ft (60.96 m) in 1912 as well as introducing the event to America. In the 1908 London Olympic Games two styles of javelin throwing were contested, one gripping the middle of the shaft, the other with a free grip, usually on the tail. Once again, Lemming dominated both events, and established the precedent of a Scandinavian dominance of this event. Another great Scandinavian, Matti Jarvinen (Finland), dominated the scene during the thirties, being possibly the first thrower successfully to blend the approach run and the delivery into one continuous and smooth movement. Of the 16 modern Olympic Games in which javelin throwing has been an event, the Scandinavians have won ten, five of those competitors coming from Finland.

In more recent decades the Scandinavians have not had it so much their own way. In 1956 Janusz Sidlo (Poland) broke the world record and went on to compete as favourite in the 1964 Tokyo Olympics. More recently two Americans, Bud and Dick Held, showed themselves as top-class competitors and both experimented to produce a javelin with better aerodynamic qualities, known as the 'Dick Held'. In 1964 Scandinavia once again figured in the world records with Pederson (Norway) becoming the first man to exceed the 300 ft (91.50 m) marker, adding 16 ft (4.87 m) to the already existing world record. In 1968, perhaps the greatest thrower of the modern era, Janis Lusis (USSR), made his mark upon the event by winning the Mexico Olympic title with a throw of 295 ft 7 in (90.10 m). He subsequently went on to win many of the medals in the top competitions.

Unlike the other throwing events, improvements in javelin throwing can rarely be attributed to improvements in technique, which has changed little since its original form. Improvements, however, have been brought about in two main areas, which could account for the longer distances: technical and training. On the technical side, improvements in the aerodynamics of the javelin, improved run-up surfaces together with the resulting improvements in footwear, have all had their effect on the event. More important, however, is the improvement in training techniques towards producing a supple and strong, more gymnast-like athlete who can combine speed and strength through optimum physical positions, in order to produce a greater application of force upon the javelin. Thus javelin throwing is no longer the province of the strong-arm throwers, long susceptible to injuries of the elbow joint, but is now for the technique conscious athlete who does more to prepare himself physically for the enormous physical strains involved in top-class competition. This attention to physical preparation will undoubtedly prolong the active career of javelin throwers, much as it did for Sidlo (Poland) whose career lasted in excess of twenty years.

SAFETY PRECAUTIONS

In order to avoid accidents, competitors must be given instructions that implements must be thrown during practice only from the scratch line or the immediate vicinity thereof and must be returned during practice or competition by hand and NOT THROWN back to the starting area. The referee or appropriate official shall disqualify from competing in the event any athlete who wilfully disobeys the above instructions after having his attention drawn to them.

This is probably the most abused rule in athletics and it is fortunate that more accidents do not occur. The javelin is a lethal weapon, hence the strictest safety precautions must be observed. In most large meetings the throwing sector is fenced off to prevent accidents and a warning hooter sounds before each throw. Those dealing with young or inexperienced athletes must teach their pupils how to carry the javelin to the throwing area. They must also be taught that both ends of the javelin are equally dangerous. In fact, in javelin throwing a lot of minor accidents occur with the tail of the javelin. Teachers and those dealing with young athletes are advised to read very carefully the precautions set out by the Schools Athletic Association in their yearly handbook, a short synopsis of which follows:

During Training: (a) To carry the implement in the correct way so that passers-by are not incommoded.
(b) To assemble all throwers, well spread, behind a scratch line.
(c) To throw in one direction only (which means no 'pair throwing' or 'return throwing').
(d) To ensure that no one crosses the scratch line until all javelins have been thrown.
(e) To retrieve all these implements on a set order and to carry them

correctly in the hand to the throwing position behind the scratch line.

Note on Landing Rule: Rule 184 section 3 of the IAAF handbook states that 'No throw shall be valid in which the tip of the metal head does not strike the ground before any other part of the javelin.' It does not say that it must stick in the ground or even make a mark. With the modern aerodynamic javelin the rule is most difficult to interpret and one wonders why the rule is there in the first place. The rules do not say that the discus must land edge first. Once the athlete has released the javelin he has no control over how it should land. Hence one finds that the judging in this event is both arbitrary and inconsistent.

Breakdown of the Event

THE GRIP

There are three main recognized grips used in javelin throwing. In all three two points may be noticed: first, the hand is situated at a point where the majority of power, and thus impetus, may be exerted against the back edge of the binding; second, the javelin never rests directly across the palm of the hand, but should lie diagonally across the palm to act as a suitable platform for the correct delivery.

The first of these grips may be called the orthodox grip, in which the thumb and first finger of the hand are placed firmly behind the edge of the binding. The second type of grip, often called the pen grip, is that in which the thumb and second finger contact the binding while the forefinger rests alongside the shaft of the javelin. The last type of grip is called the horseshoe, in which the javelin rests in the V formed by the first and second fingers. Choice of grip often depends upon the size and strength of the athlete's hand, although often such choice may more reasonably be dictated by comfort and feel. Peter's own choice is for the orthodox grip because it is the most natural of the three, although many coaches feel that the horseshoe grip is often more effective for delivery.

The remaining fingers of the hand wrap firmly across the binding in order to ensure the correct angle of release. Many athletes feel that the positioning of the fingers causes the javelin to spin, thus aiding stability for flight; this, however, is purely incidental and should not form part of the intention of the athlete.

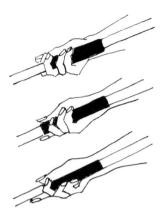

THE CARRY

Much controversy has surrounded the method by which the javelin is carried during the run-up. Only two fundamental principles should be adhered to in the chosen method: first that it is performed in such a manner that it will not impede a smooth running action; secondly that it is comfortable for the athlete himself. In our opinion, the most efficient method of carrying the javelin is to hold it at a position

directly over the throwing shoulder. Whether it points upward or downward matters very little, unless excessive, provided that on the withdrawal it achieves an optimum position. It should be noted that the shoulders, and the arms should be as relaxed as much as the technique will permit.

The Approach Run

Unlike the other throwing events, in javelin the athlete is permitted an unlimited length of run-up. The major principle governing the length of the run-up is that, at the point immediately prior to delivery, the athlete has achieved his maximum amount of speed with the minimum of necessary effort and the maximum of control. Only through experience can the athlete acquire a measured distance suitable to his ability to achieve the correct run-up.

As with gymnastic vaulters and athletic pole vaulters, the athlete may choose to measure this run-up—having decided the measurement through experience—and place a check mark at his starting point. The acceleration into the approach-run should be gradual and rhythmical and the length of stride should be reasonably controlled. There should be no sudden variation in stride pattern in order to hit other check marks that the athlete may choose to have next to the runway.

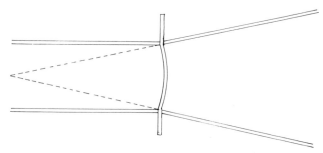

A check mark is positioned towards the end of the approach run. This enables the athlete to determine the point at which he can move into the transition phase, in the knowledge that he will utilize all the runway without fear of fouling the throwing line.

The Transition

(a) *Withdrawal:* this phase of the throw commences when the right foot hits the second check mark and is completed within three strides. During these three strides the object is to take the javelin back to a point where it is withdrawn to its maximum extension behind the desired line of throw.

As the left foot contacts the ground, the shoulders start to turn and the throwing arm begins to extend backward. This extension is fully completed by the time the left foot next contacts the ground and should be performed as smoothly as possible. Once the throwing arm is fully extended, the shoulders should have turned so that the left shoulder now points directly towards the line of throw. Our own preference is to withdraw the arm in a straight line from a point directly above the right shoulder, so that the tip of javelin arrives at a position next to the right side of the head and at eye level. The left arm should be wrapped across the chest in order to ensure that excess muscular tension is reduced.

While this movement is being performed the athlete should attempt to keep his hips as square to the direction of throw as possible so there is no loss of speed in this part of the run-up. The demand for a supple back is therefore probably greater for the javelin thrower than for other throwers.

Once the javelin has been fully withdrawn it should lie across the palm and close beside the throwing arm with the hand at a position slightly below shoulder level. The athlete should ensure that, at this point, the tail of the javelin does not drop too far or this will be so increased on 'lay-back' that it might touch the ground.

(b) *The Cross-over Stride:* as the right foot hits the second check mark, the cross-over stride and lay-back phase is begun. The primary aim of this phase is to get the body into a position where the majority of weight is leaning back over the right foot, in a bow position, so that the large muscles of the upper body are used efficiently in the delivery phase. The classic cross-over stride resulted in the hips turning away from a direction facing square to the throwing area and involved a movement with the right leg actually crossing in front of the left. Today, this is no longer favoured as it is regarded as being less efficient than a technique which will allow the hips to face square to the throwing area, ensuring better hip displacement throughout.

In the more conventional technique of today only the shoulders are rotated at the point where the right foot hits the check mark. The left foot then takes an extended stride and, as it contacts the ground, the right knee executes an extremely fast pick up, causing the athlete momentarily to break contact with the ground, with the left leg trailing behind. So the cross-over occurs in the air and, in order to attain an effective body lean, the athlete must attempt to get his right heel back on to the ground as fast as possible. The right foot makes contact with the ground with the toes facing approximately 80-degrees away from the direction of throw. One should notice that no actual cross-over has occurred as would have been executed in the classic technique and that the heel of the right foot contacts the ground first in preparation for the throwing stride.

The athlete at this point is in a position with his weight moving on to his right foot; his left leg trailing behind and his body is leant backward with the throwing arm now fully extended behind him. With the athlete now in a lay-back position, and with his weight being behind the right heel, the right leg is slightly flexed as the left leg is pulled through, executing a long stabbing action to ensure a wide base. Immediately before the left heel makes contact with the ground, the right leg begins its drive and pivots around the ball of the foot so that the knee turns inward to face the line of throw. As the left heel contacts the ground the leg is perfectly straight, but as the athlete moves from the lay-back position forward towards the delivery phase, this left leg flexes slightly before bracing straight once more to act as a 'hinge' on delivery.

Throughout the cross-over and throwing stride it may be noticed that the hips are kept as square to the line of throw as possible in order to ensure that the athlete performs a more natural type of running action. The fact that only the shoulders turn in this technique ensures the generation of extra torque on the hips, coupled with a more effective lay-back, and subsequent bow, position.

THE DELIVERY
With the left leg slightly flexed and the left foot firmly in contact with the ground, the athlete has begun to drive off the right foot pushing the right knee and hip forward so that the body is forced into an extreme bow position. It is the driving action of the right leg which forces the right hip forward and upward by acting against the bracing action of the left leg. The combined action of the left braced leg and the right driving leg produces considerable rotation of the upper body

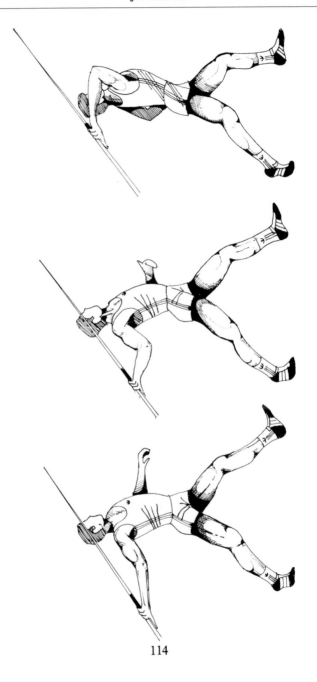

114

around the vertical axis. This rotation causes the chest and right shoulder to turn square to the direction of throw, while the head looks up towards the line of throw.

As the right hip punches square to the direction of the throw, the previously passive right throwing arm comes into action. It is our opinion that as the left foot contacts the ground, the throwing arm should not be held in a fully extended and locked position but should at this point be slightly bent. This slight bend should automatically result from the punching action of the hips and the turn of the shoulders. It should not form part of the intention of the athlete, nor should it be the intention of the athlete to keep the arm locked straight. As the shoulders turn to the front the elbow rotates outward, but not away from the body. From this point onward the athlete must attempt to keep the elbow high and as close to the shoulder as possible.

The pull of the throwing arm occurs simultaneously with the thrust of the right hip and the twist of the trunk, and is completed with the bracing of the left leg. The throwing arm is whipped forward with the elbow leading the right hand so that the javelin is propelled forward in a straight line close to the right ear. As the pull is completed, the left leg and side become fully braced, and the rotation of the right hip is also completed. As the right hand passes over the shoulder and close to the right ear, the body should now be in an almost vertical position with the weight being transferred forward on to the toe. From this point onward the arm continues to unleash until it is in an extended position with the fingers pointing along the line of flight; thus the complete action of the arm is in the fashion of a whiplash.

From the point where the shoulders start to turn square towards the direction of throw, the left arm is held passively curled in front of the chest. As the shoulders start to turn, this arm sweeps outward and away to the left, but remaining flexed. By locking this left shoulder and arm at the point where the javelin is being pulled the athlete can help to prevent over-rotation at the point of delivery.

THE RECOVERY

With the javelin having now left the hand, the major problem for the athlete is to halt all forward momentum in order not to foul the line. There is no formal technique for the recovery itself, although it may be noticed that many athletes release the javelin some distance before the line in order to leave room to operate some method of recovery.

On delivery, Peter prefers to take a step forward on an extended right leg and, as this contacts the ground, he allows the left leg to swing upward and straight so that it executes a wide arc. Simultaneously, he allows his upper body to bend forward while the right leg flexes to absorb any remaining forward momentum.

1   2

3

4

5

6

7

8

Faults and Corrective Procedures

1. *Incorrect hand hold:* It is often the case that the javelin is gripped so firmly as to cause it to lie directly across the palm of the hand, rather than to be merely 'platformed' diagonally across the hand. This results in the point of the javelin wandering away from the line of the throw in the approach run and in the withdrawal phase, resulting in diversification upon delivery.

The athlete should ensure that the javelin is platformed by the palm of the hand and that it lies along a line running (approximately) from the base of the forefinger down to the left, outer edge of the wrist. He should also ensure that the javelin is not gripped too hard by the fingers in such a way as to cause it to deviate from this position.

2. *Incorrect withdrawal of the throwing arm:* The most common fault in the withdrawal phase is for the athlete to withdraw the javelin out to the side and low down, which results in the javelin being inclined at too great an angle for delivery. With the point being held too high, the result is often that the tail makes contact with the ground on lay-back, giving an incorrect angle of delivery on release. This is usually caused by the athlete failing to withdraw the right arm from a point above the right shoulder straight back and behind him so that the point of the javelin comes to a position at eye level.

The athlete should ensure that the throwing arm does not drop away from the shoulder to his side, and he should also ensure that he can see the point of the javelin out of the corner of his eye when it has been fully withdrawn. If the fault persists he should return to the practice of standing throws, which commence at the withdrawal phase, and check the angle of the javelin immediately prior to delivery.

3. *Failing to extend the right arm during the withdrawal phase:* This usually occurs as a result of a lack of suppleness in the right shoulder and may therefore need remedial training for the athlete to be able to achieve this position comfortably. However, it may also occur because the athlete is anxious to move into the delivery phase as quickly as possible and may be a result of incorrect timing of the withdrawal.

Failing to extend the right arm fully during the withdrawal phase causes the athlete to reduce the range of his pull on the javelin, as well as causing increased muscular tension in the throwing arm due to its faulty positioning. Although a fully extended arm is advocated, the extension should be relaxed and not one of tension. Relaxed muscles move faster ensuring the correct whiplash action of the arm, with the resulting explosive pull on the javelin.

An ideal practice to ensure a good feel of this position is to adopt a lay-back position, with the arm fully extended, and to allow someone to hold the end of the javelin while you operate the technique with your hip and shoulder. Thus the right leg, hip, and shoulder commence the delivery while the arm remains almost passive until finally it comes into play.

4. *Insufficient lay-back before delivery:* There is a natural tendency for athletes to attempt to maintain a normal upright running position throughout this part of the technique. This occurs either because the athlete is endeavouring to maintain forward momentum of the upper body, in which case the athlete feels that the lay-back slows him down, or because he is anxious to get into the delivery phase as quickly as possible.

Failing to achieve sufficient lay-back results in some, or all, of the following: reduces range of pull on the javelin; failure to plant the left heel prior to delivery; failure to achieve a bow position; inability of the right leg to perform an effective drive; unbalanced delivery leading to fouling. Once again the athlete may revert to a standing throw in order to feel the lay-back position and then progress to walking into the lay-back position, and onward to the full technique.

5. *Narrow base upon delivery:* This fault occurs in the throwing stride where the athlete fails to extend his left leg sufficiently far enough forward to provide a wide base between both feet. This results in: an ineffective, or short, pull of the right hip into the delivery; inefficient drive of the right leg; excess forward momentum resulting from possible failure of the left leg to brace straight. To correct this fault the athlete should concentrate on extending his left leg, in the throwing stride, so that the heel contacts the ground after an *extended* stride.

6. *Poor arm delivery:* The most common fault is a failure of the elbow to pass close to the right ear during delivery so that the arm performs the correct whiplash action. The athlete should bear this point in mind as

he operates the throwing sequence: right leg, hip, shoulder, elbow and wrist. This may also occur as a result of a failure to invert the elbow (inwardly rotate) during the pulling action of the arm. The major consequence of this fault, apart from incorrect delivery, is often injury to the elbow or shoulder, usually painful and often permanent. Therefore, one should pay particular attention to the remedy of this fault.

7. *Throwing off the back leg:* Many athletes often fail to deliver the javelin when the weight is moving over the front foot. This usually occurs, either because the athlete braces his left leg too early, or because his feet have formed a small base from which to drive—making it imperative to brace the left leg early to avoid falling forward. The athlete must ensure that he establishes the correct base prior to delivery and that he times the bracing of the left leg at the point when his weight is moving on to it.

8. *Incorrect delivery:* Many faults can occur at delivery, but the most common of these faults is over-rotation, the athlete turning away from the direction of throw prior to releasing the javelin. Although there are many things which may cause this to happen, the two most common faults which we have observed are the premature turning of the head away from the direction of throw, and a breaking of the left hip which causes the shoulders to over-rotate. Both of these faults, and they are often combined, result in a divergence of the javelin from its correct line of flight. If the athlete is over-rotating by breaking at the left hip, than he has failed to make use of the fulcrum provided by his braced left leg. He should therefore ensure that the whole of his left side remains locked and that he is looking towards the direction of throw on delivery.

Training to Throw the Javelin

In the development of javelin throwing it has become increasingly apparent that height and weight are not the only desirable physical qualities for top performance. The physical attributes required are far more akin to those of a gymnast: strength with speed; extreme agility; suppleness. The athlete must develop the ability to accelerate to maximum speed over a distance of 30 m (27½ yd) and, while maintaining his momentum, he must perform several actions requiring a high degree of agility and suppleness. Finally, he must apply his maximum strength with maximum speed in order to achieve optimum performance.

SUITABLE EXERCISES FOR STRENGTH

Abdominal Exercises: due to the excessive bow position, which the javelin thrower achieves immediately prior to delivery and the subsequent range through which he must apply his power, strength in the abdominal region is vitally important.

Any exercise which involves lying on one's back and performing a piking action at the waist is ideal for fostering abdominal strength (either free-standing or using weights). A more specific exercise is to lie on the back with the feet being anchored in some manner while gripping a medicine ball which is on the floor behind your head, and then to attempt to throw the ball as far forward as possible by sitting up into the throw.

Pull-overs: lie on a bench with your feet flat on the floor. Hold a weighted bar with straight arms over your chest (as for bench press). From this position three types of pull-overs may be performed:

First, with straight arms throughout, lower the bar backward to a position level with the top of your head, and then return to the starting position above the chest.

Second, bending the arms and keeping the elbows as close together as possible lower the bar backward as far as you can, and then return to the starting position by straightening at the elbow (ensuring that the elbows remain in one position). Last, as for the second exercise, lower the bar backwards by bending at the elbow, but instead of straightening the arms, merely pull the bar back to a position where it rests on top of the chest (maintaining bent arms throughout).

Tricep Extensions: sit on the edge of a bench and lower a weighted bar downward, behind your neck, until both arms are fully bent with the elbows held high and backward. From this position, and without moving your elbows, raise the weight above the back of your head until your arms are fully extended, then lower to original position. This exercise is similar to pull-overs, except that it is performed in a sitting position and may also be performed by the throwing arm alone.

Trunk Circling: for this exercise the athlete hangs from a bar or rings and, maintaining straight knees, circles his legs as far left as possible, then upward as high as possible, and then gently lowers them to his right back to the original position. The exercise is then repeated by circling in the opposite direction. This is an ideal exercise for strengthening the sides and lower abdomen, so vital for the explosive power demanded during the delivery phase.

SUITABLE EXERCISES FOR SUPPLING

Dislocations: standing with his back to a fixed bar, the athlete secures an overhand grip with his arms extended behind him. By pushing his hips and chest forward and head backward, his arms, still maintaining their grip, circle to the front. This exercise may also be performed using the javelin itself, the athlete remaining in an upright standing position while the shoulders and arms perform the circling action. In both exercises the athlete attempts to perform the complete movement with his hands as close together as possible.

Hanging from Rings: for this exercise the athlete takes a grip on the rings and turns over in a circling motion, to hang fully relaxed with his arms extended upward behind him. If he maintains a stiff body, this exercise can be further enhanced if a partner gently lifts him until he reaches a position where he may press the rings outward and forward, in a circling motion to the front (dislocation).

SPEED

More than any other athletic thrower, the javelin thrower requires a good sprinting ability. Unlike any other athlete, this sprinting ability should only be developed over a distance of approximately 30 metres. Anything in excess of that is unnecessary to the actual technique. Any sprint training which will develop his ability to reach maximum speed over this distance will suffice. It must be remembered that his sprinting action will be inhibited by the fact that he has to carry, and deliver, a javelin, therefore any sprint training must be quickly related to his actual event if it is to have great value.

Stamina and Planned Training

For details on these aspects of training please refer to the relevant parts of earlier chapters.

Peter Tancred's Competitive Career

DISCUS
UK Teenage record holder 1968 under 18—175 ft 11 in (53.62 m)
UK Teenage record holder 1969 under 19—188 ft 10 in (57.56 m)
Competitor: European Games (Athens) 1969
           Olympic Games (Montreal) 1976
           European Cup Finals 1977
           Commonwealth Games (Edmonton) 1978
British Champion 1977 and 1978
Numerous international appearances since 1968—current GB international competitor
World's best brothers duo, with Bill Tancred—211 ft 0 in (64.31 m)
Peter Tancred—202 ft 2 in (61.62 m)
No. 2 on UK All-time List (second only to Bill Tancred up to end of 1978)

SHOT
AAA Junior Champion 1968
International competitor (indoors and outdoors) 1974 and 1976
Runner-up in the British Indoor Championships 1974 and 1976

HAMMER
International competitor 1977

JAVELIN
3rd All-England Championships (under 15) 1964